C000302286

First published 2018

The History Press
The Mill, Brimscombe Port
Stroud, Gloucestershire, GL5 2QG
www.thehistorypress.co.uk

© David Ramshaw, 2018

The right of David Ramshaw to be identified as the Author
of this work has been asserted in accordance with the
Copyright, Designs and Patents Act 1988.

All rights reserved. No part of this book may be reprinted
or reproduced or utilised in any form or by any electronic,
mechanical or other means, now known or hereafter invented,
including photocopying and recording, or in any information
storage or retrieval system, without the permission in writing
from the Publishers.

British Library Cataloguing in Publication Data.
A catalogue record for this book is available from the British Library.

ISBN 978 0 7509 8479 9

Typesetting and origination by The History Press
Printed and bound in Great Britain by TJ International Ltd, Padstow, Cornwall

CONTENTS

ABOUT THE AUTHOR

David Ramshaw is an author and local publisher. He began writing Lakeland guides with local history in the 1990s and has since won several 'Lakeland Book of the Year' awards. David has walked the Lake District for more than sixty years and has a wealth of interesting tales to tell. He is a committee member for the Outdoor Writers and Photographers Guild. David has an honours degree in physics and chemistry and taught physics for more than thirty years. He lives in Carlisle.

INTRODUCTION

Cumbria stands out from many other counties in England in that the terrain is very varied. There is the flat marshy land of the Solway Plain, with coastal towns and villages lining the shores of the Solway estuary. Inland there are remote and sometimes inaccessible fells, valleys and lakes, which form the central part of the area. Further east the land becomes friendlier with the rolling hills and fertile farmland of the Eden Valley. This remote area in the far north of England has attracted settlers for thousands of years, often for very different reasons.

After the last Ice Age it became home to Neolithic people, who lived in forts on the hilltops and foraged in the forests below. They eventually became the early farmers, who defended their mountainous land from other tribal groups. Then, 2,000 years ago, the Romans invaded to conquer and civilise England, reaching well into Scotland where they built the Antonine Wall; from the Clyde to the Forth. It might be said that this was a 'wall too far' and in AD 100 their frontier was brought back to Cumberland and Hadrian built his sea-to-sea wall from Bowness in the west to Wallsend in the east. He apparently decided that the lands to the north, occupied by the Picts, were just not worth the trouble of attempting further conquest.

After the Romans departed, chaos reigned again as the Saxon south tried to conquer the northern parts of England, leading to a depopulation of the area. This was soon remedied by Viking invaders, mainly from the Isle of Man. The Norsemen liked this land, which reminded them of home and, over the years, they settled in with the local population; resulting in our present native Cumbrian people. Further attempts to conquer Cumberland came after the Norman invasion with the building of castles around this mountainous land. However, the Normans were not successful in this endeavour and eventually they gave the area to the King of Scotland to govern.

By the fifteenth and sixteenth centuries the area immediately to the north and east of the Solway had become real bandit country, known as the 'debatable lands'. Here the Border reiver families held sway, feuding amongst themselves and their neighbours, rustling cattle and sheep, killing, kidnapping and extorting protection money. This past lawlessness of the area is evidenced by the large number of fortified farmhouses and pele towers still to be found. The area only became really settled in Elizabethan times, apart from the Civil War and the 1745 rebellion, which caused some disruption to normal living.

Cumbria is best known, of course, for the Lake District National Park that falls within its boundaries, arguably the most scenic area of England and now awarded UNESCO World Heritage status. The Lake District has attracted visitors for hundreds of years with its narrow valleys, its lakes and tarns, all enclosed by steep-sided mountains. Poets such as Wordsworth and Coleridge lived here and in Victorian times it became known as 'the nursery of the alps', as many of our early climbers and walkers gained their expertise in the Lakeland hills. The author has spent most of his life in the area, teaching, walking, exploring the mines, cycling and, since retiring, writing guidebooks and local history books.

Cumbria has a rich history of human occupation and development, enough to fill a hundred books. In this 'little book of Cumbria' the intention is to entertain the reader with interesting and amusing information about the inhabitants, the places where they lived, their folklore and their relationship with the land over the years.

David Ramshaw, 2018

1

THE NORTH-WESTERN PART OF THE COUNTY

ASPATRIA

Spatrie, as pronounced by the locals, or Aspatria is an ancient settlement and seems to have been home to a group of Norsemen who fled to the area from Ireland around AD 900. In 1789, a surgeon by the name of Mr Rigg employed a group of labourers to level a mound called Beacon Hill, situated close behind his house at Aspatria. After reaching a depth of about 1m they dug into a cavity walled around with large stones and found the skeleton of a Viking chief, almost complete and more than 2m long. At the head of the gigantic skeleton lay a sword of similar size, with a remarkably broad blade, ornamented with a gold and silver handle. The scabbard of the sword was made of wood, lined with cloth. The workmen also unearthed several pieces of armour, a dirk with a silver-studded handle, a golden-buckled belt, and a breastplate. The artefacts are in the British Museum. The village stands at the northern end of the West Cumberland Coalfield and there have been mines in the area since the sixteenth century. However, the last pit in the town closed in 1940.

WIGTON

The Romans had a cavalry station, Maglona, known locally as Old Carlisle, just to the south of the town with a large civilian settlement. From here they could react to incursions from north of Hadrian's Wall. After Roman rule, Wigton was within the native British kingdom of Rheged, most likely of Anglian origin. Wigton and most of Cumberland were a part of Scotland in 1086 when the Domesday Book was written for William I, so are not included in it.

GEORGE MOORE

The most famous son of Wigton is George Moore, merchant, millionaire and philanthropist. In 1825, aged 19, George left rural Wigton to make his fortune in London. After several weeks of looking for work and being rejected he seriously considered emigrating to America. Then he was told to get in touch with a Cumberland man, Mr Ray, a partner in the firm of Flint, Ray and Co., haberdashers of Soho Square. Mr Ray came from an old Cumberland family who owned Lesson Hall near Wigton for many generations. Cumbrians in exile are a loyal clan, and Mr Ray immediately offered George accommodation and employment at £30 a year. Many years later, a fellow employee of Mr Ray commented that George 'was the most unlikely lad in England to have made the great future that he did'. Throughout his years as a commercial traveller George put in relentless hours covering the length and

Eliza's Memorial.

breadth of the country. His ethics were so clean and his standards so high that his friend Charles Dickens, no less, portrayed him as the eponymous lead character in his collection of literary sketches and reminiscences, *The Uncommercial Traveller*.

George never forgot his native Cumberland. In 1857, now very rich, and recently widowed, he bought Whitehall, the scene of his wild and carefree boyhood. This he renovated over the next few years.

George erected a splendid memorial to his wife, Eliza, in the form of a fountain, which still stands in the centre of Wigton.

During his lifetime, George Moore gave away a fortune to establish training opportunities for young men, to set up libraries, and to enhance the work of schools and hospitals. Even after his death the bequests listed in his will, granted to around sixty charities and to family members, totalled around £220,000. Today that would be equivalent to £18.7 million. George died by accident in English Street, Carlisle, at the age of 70. A horse bolted free from livery stables in Lonsdale Street and careered wildly up Bank Street and into English Street, where George was standing outside the Grey Goat Inn (where House of Fraser stands today). The passing animal felled him to the pavement. He was carried into the inn and died soon after.

South of Aspatria and Wigton lies Bassenthwaite Lake, to the north of Keswick and bounded by the mountain of Skiddaw to the east at 931m (3,054ft). Bassenthwaite is noted for being the home of Britain's rarest freshwater fish, the vendace. More than ten years ago it was declared as being 'locally extinct' until it made an unexpected reappearance in Derwentwater in 2013, then the only known remaining native habitat for this fish. However, in autumn 2016, a fish community survey of Bassenthwaite Lake recorded a single young vendace specimen.

The reader may be surprised to be told that Bassenthwaite Lake is the only lake in the Lake District. Surely you have all heard the question posed by many jokers in the past: 'How many lakes are there in the Lake District?' Answer: 'One, Bassenthwaite Lake. All the rest are waters or meres, of course.'

As one travels north from Keswick on the A66, the steep slate scree slope of Barf is seen to the left with a large white-painted rock standing near the top of the scree. This is the Bishop of Barf, a memorial to a foolish wager. In 1783 the newly appointed Bishop of Derry, now Londonderry, was in the area and stayed at the Swan Hotel in Thornthwaite (now unfortunately closed, called Swan House, privately owned and part let as holiday accommodation). He wagered that he would ride his horse up the side of Barf and onwards to the summit of Lord's Seat. Unfortunately, on attempting this feat, his horse fell on reaching the height of Bishop Rock, killing both horse and rider. The bishop was laid to rest at the base of the mountain and to commemorate his rather foolhardy enterprise the rock, known as the Bishop's

Bishop Rock.

D·LUSH.

Clerk, was painted white by patrons of the Swan, who maintain the bishop in his pristine white coat to this very day. Since the hotel closed, local villagers have continued this tradition. The fee paid to patrons painting the rock was set at one shilling and a quart of ale.

OSPREYS AT WHINLATTER

Whinlatter Forest, immediately to the south and west of Barf, is a great recreation area for visitors with all the usual facilities provided by the Forestry Commission for the public. However, in April 2001 Whinlatter became the first place in the Lake District where ospreys successfully bred. We know for certain that ospreys have not bred in the Lake District for at least 150 years. From 1916 onwards ospreys passed through Cumbria when migrating and they did breed (more or less undetected) in Scotland between 1916 and 1954, when a pair bred successfully on Speyside, the now famous Loch Garten site.

In 1998 it was decided to build a number of artificial nest sites at Whinlatter. Mating was observed on one of these sites in 2000. Very few people were aware of this. Even fewer people were aware that, in 1999, an osprey nested near the River Eden, south of Carlisle. However, the breeding failed at the egg stage. These birds returned in 2000 and successfully reared a single chick, the first in Cumbria for at least 170 years and the first recorded in England since 1842. This led to the formation of the Lake District Osprey Project in 2000 from three organisations: the Lake District National Park Authority, the Forestry Commission and the RSPB.

The birds returned in April 2001, as did the start of their protection. Foot-and-mouth disease ravaged Cumbria, an advantage and a disadvantage. Staff were released from other duties, making around the clock protection easier but due to animal welfare restrictions, access was difficult at the best watch points.

In those early days the top of Barf was an ideal site (kept quiet at the time) to watch the ospreys on their nest from above, until in April 2008, they decided to nest on the other side of the lake on a previously prepared artificial nest. Since then the official viewpoint has been on the lower slopes of Skiddaw Dodd. At the time of writing in 2017 a total of twenty-six chicks have fledged at Whinlatter, a great success story and a great tourist attraction.

THE EMBLETON SWORD

Embleton is the small village under Ling Fell between Keswick and Cockermouth. In the early part of the nineteenth century a Celtic sword, known as the Embleton Sword, was found in a field adjacent to Wythop Mill near the great stone, thought to be the site of an ancient battleground. The sword was in its sheath ornamented with enamels of various colours. It was placed in the Peter Crosthwaite Museum, Keswick, but it eventually found its way to the British Museum. It is believed to date from 50 BC and is probably the best example of its kind in Britain. In 1985, on hearing that the sword was miles from its ancestral home, three apprentices at Workington's British Steel plant determined to make a steel replica. The sword was forged by the apprentices and the scabbard was made and decorated by Mrs P. Beaty of Cockermouth. In April of that year the replica sword, a truly beautiful object, was handed over to the village at a ceremony in St Cuthbert's Church, where it now resides.

D. LUSH.

Embleton Sword.

CORPSE ROAD FROM WYTHOP/ EMBLETON AND LORTON

The inhabitants of Wythop and Lorton talk about an ancient corpse road that linked the two villages. One story is that in the past there was no burial ground at Wythop, as Wythop was a township and chapelry within the parish of Lorton, and coffins were transported on horseback to High Lorton for internment. This is supported by the fact that some of the pews at Lorton Church were marked 'Wythop Pews'. The route wound its way through Burthwaite, around the edge of Wythop Moss, over Widow Hause via Darling How and Skawgill Bridge to High Lorton. The name Widow Hause on the OS map gives this route some credence. It is supposed to be possible to see the raised stone resting places for the coffins along the route, but the author has yet to find them.

A possible alternative route is the well-graded path traversing the northern slope of Ling Fell and labelled Corpse Road on the modern OS map (Copse Road on the older versions). This route is more direct, although it does climb rather high up the fell and becomes indistinct at Tom Rudd beck.

KELSWICK CHAPEL

The remains of the old chapel, built in 1473, are still to be seen alongside the track that passes through Chapel Wood below Sale Fell. Chapel Wood is said to be the oldest surviving oak planting in the British Isles. The chapel, rebuilt in 1673, had no vestry, chancel, turret or spire. There was no font or burial ground, hence the need for a corpse road. The Wythop church bell hung in a tree near the east window. This had the disadvantage that the church bell would toll whenever there were gales, striking fear into the God-fearing local farmers. The church fell into disuse in the eighteenth century and was pulled down in 1865. For many years a church service has been held at the site of the old chapel on the third Sunday in August.

SILICA BRICKWORKS (SHARE PUFFING SCANDAL)

The visitor walking the remote track past Wythop Hall towards Beck Wythop may wonder at the signs of past industrial activity presented by the remains of the old silica brickworks. This was an ill-fated venture to produce fire bricks from the local quartz rock. A share prospectus to raise £120,000 was floated in 1932 and the building of the works provided work for fifty men over a two-year period. The plant, including kilns, a very tall chimney and a crusher, was duly completed with an overhead cableway being commenced to link the crusher with the quarry. Meanwhile, the kilns were fired up and about 50 tons of bricks produced in the first few days. Alas, that was all that was ever produced! On the next firing the kilns were somehow overheated and they all collapsed. This was rather fortunate for the instigators of the venture as it turned out there were no workable reserves of quartz in the area. No local money was involved. People the author has spoken with locally maintain that everyone, including the directors, knew the venture was not viable and that it was an example of a swindle known as 'share puffing'. The works have since been pulled down and all that remains are the foundations of the plant and, in the forest, the plinths for the proposed cableway.

FLOODS IN NORTH-WEST CUMBRIA

Keswick, Cockermouth and Workington hit the headlines in November 2009 when the worst floods in living memory hit the towns. The greatest disruption occurred in Cockermouth. The River Cocker joins the River Derwent in the middle of the town so that the watershed from both the Lorton and the Derwent valleys met here, 'reared up', overtopped the banks and flooded large areas of the town before travelling onwards to Workington, where all the bridges were destroyed or damaged. In particular, the main road bridge connecting North and South Workington was washed away, resulting in the tragic death of PC Bill Barker, who was warning people to keep off the bridge when it suddenly collapsed under him. Continuous rain over the whole catchment at that time was the cause and it was later deemed to be a once-in-1,000-year flood. Yet, in spite of millions being spent on flood defences since then, in 2015, only six years later, these new defences were overtopped once more in all three towns, as well as in Carlisle. This book is being written in the summer of 2017 and there are still people who have not yet been able to return to their homes.

Cockermouth owes its name and existence to the river system. The nearby Roman camp of Dervenitio, modern Papcastle, was situated at the northern end of a crossing of the River Derwent, which flows from east to west just north of the present town centre. This was an important road junction in the support to Hadrian's Wall. Other Roman forts are scattered along the coast from the end of the wall at Bowness, at Maryport, at Ravenglass and inland at Hardknott Pass. Nowadays Cockermouth is an attractive market town, very popular with walkers, exploring the north-western hills. The town is also famous for its association with various well-known people. The poet William Wordsworth was born here and, surprisingly, two other famous people were born in the small village of Eaglesfield, only a couple of miles south of the town. One was the mutineer Fletcher Christian, and the other was the father of atomic theory, John Dalton.

Dalton was a keen meteorologist, which involved a lot of mountain climbing: until the advent of aeroplanes and weather balloons, the only way to make measurements of temperature and humidity at altitude was to climb a mountain. Dalton was often accompanied by Jonathan Otley (mentioned elsewhere in this book), who was one of the few authorities on the heights of the Lake District mountains. John Dalton climbed Helvellyn once a year for about forty years, in his words: 'to bring into exercise a set of muscles which would otherwise have grown stiff'. Once, caught in mist, they were slowly descending when Dalton exclaimed: 'Not one step more! There is nothing but mist to tread on!' Thus he saved the party above Red Tarn.

Travelling south into Lorton Vale, the next village encountered is Low Lorton next to the River Cocker. High Lorton adjoins above and to the east and, as its name suggests, is safe from flooding, unlike its neighbour. High Lorton is famous for the Lorton Yew, described by Wordsworth as follows:

THE PRIDE OF LORTON VALE

There is a yew-tree, pride of Lorton Vale,
Which to this day stands single, in the midst
Of its own darkness, as it stood of yore:
(...)
Of vast circumference and gloom profound
This solitary tree! a living thing
Produced too slowly ever to decay;
Of form and aspect too magnificent
To be destroyed.

This poem probably saved the tree. In 1898 Edmund Bogg described the tree as being 'now only a wreck of its former glory'. He continues:

In its pride and strength the trunk measured twenty four feet in circumference; one of its own branches was some years ago wrenched off right down to the ground. At another time the tree was actually sold for fifteen pounds to a cabinet maker from Whitehaven, and two men began to stub it up, but fortunately a gentleman from Cockermouth, hearing of its proposed destruction, made overtures to the owner, and thus preserved, though shorn of its ancient dignity, the pride of Lorton Vale.

The tree can still be seen today on the green behind the village hall in High Lorton. Incidentally, the large barn-like building, which is now the village hall, was originally a bobbin mill and later a well-known local brewery now based in Cockermouth.

DEATHS IN A FLOOD AT LOWESWATER AND OTHER DISASTERS

Further down the valley is Loweswater with Crabtree Beck flowing into it from Loweswater Fell above. There have been many lives lost over the years in the district due to both natural and man-made calamities. One such happening was recounted by Edmund Bogg in 1902:

Many years ago a small reservoir, or tarn, on the hill above the lake, burst, and came rolling in one huge wave towards the lake; a farm stood in its path, and one of the occupants, a girl who was outside the house, saw the dark mass of water sweeping downwards. Darting into the house, she informed the inmates (the master and a female) of the occurrence. These two had just reached the outside of the door in their endeavour to escape, when the wave caught them both, swept them into the lake, and their bodies were never discovered, whilst strange to say, the girl, who was first to discover the inundation, was saved by the water forcibly banging the door in her face and holding her prisoner, when she was in the act of following the other persons.

Recently, while researching for another book, the author came across a contemporary newspaper account of the event. It differs considerably from Edmund Bogg's version, which was presumably handed down by word of mouth over a seventy-year period:

Carlisle Journal, 26 July 1828 (abridged):

We mentioned last week that a man and his child had been drowned in the neighbourhood of one of our lakes, during the late heavy rains. The accident occurred at Crabtree beck, in Loweswater; ... A dam for supplying the lead mine with water, ... owing to the very great pressure, as it was much swollen by the heavy rains, suddenly burst, about six - o - clock in the morning of the 13th inst.; ... the whole body of water rushed in a torrent, and with a noise resembling thunder, down a steep, rocky and ragged gill, tearing up the largest trees by their roots and carrying before it everything that opposed its progress – even rocks and stones from half a ton to a ton weight! ... a servant girl, hearing the roar of the waters, had only just time to enter the house. At the same instant, Mr Tirril, her master, ... ran out of the house with the child in his arms, when both were swept away, and were never again seen! ... Mr Tirril was a man much respected in his circle, and had been married only eighteen months. Mrs Tirril, who was in bed, escaped. The bodies of the unfortunate sufferers have not yet been found.

The newspaper article is much more likely to be an accurate version of the event. It is interesting to see that Bogg talks about 'the master and a female' leaving the house. He does not mention that the female is a child in arms or the wife, still in her bed.

Further down the valley to the south is Brackenthwaite, near Lanthwaite Green, where the local Cumbrians are reputed to have fought an indecisive battle with the Normans before conquering them a few weeks later in the Battle of Rannerdale.

ERUPTION OF WHITESIDE

In recent years Cumbria has experienced the occasional ground tremor, indicating that some geological activity still exists in the area. However, if contemporary records are to be believed, these pale into insignificance when compared to the eruption of Whiteside in 1908 (Whiteside is the mountain directly above and to the east of Brackenthwaite). In July and August of that year the local people experienced a series of frightening rumblings and shakings of the ground over a three-week period. The source of the disturbance was eventually located as coming from within Whiteside. Then, on the evening of 14 August, as W.C. Hope of Cornhow was leading hay, Whiteside spoke again. The mountain gave a great moaning rumble and instinctively Mr Hope looked over at it. He got the shock of his life when he saw what looked like a great cloud of smoke rising. Then, through the cloud, came bounding a number of large boulders, which he thought had been shaken off the side of the mountain. Whiteside has not erupted again since that day and no satisfactory explanation of its long-protracted rumblings has ever been given, although it was suggested that they might be the sign of a slumbering volcano beginning to stir once more. So perhaps you should not linger too long on Whiteside.

WATERSPOUT OF 1760

John Gilpin in his book *Observations Relative Chiefly to Picturesque Beauty* (1772) describes a terrible 'waterspout', possibly a cloudburst, which devastated the area on 9 September 1760 around midnight. The waterspout originated high on the watershed of Grasmoor, sweeping down the steep valley between Grasmoor and Whiteside, in Gilpin's words:

> charging itself with all the rubbish it found there it made its way into the vale. At the foot of the mountain it was received by a piece of arable ground on which its violence first broke. Here it tore away trees, soil and gravel; and laid bare, many feet in depth to the naked rock. Over the next ten acres it seems to have made an immense roll; covering them with so vast a bed of stones that no human art can ever again restore the soil. When we saw the place, though twelve years after the event, many marks remained, still flagrant of this scene of ruin.

Gilpin goes on to describe how the village of Brackenthwaite had a wonderful escape from catastrophe as the current was deflected by a projection of the native rock on which the houses were built. The energy of the deluge was finally dissipated in the River Cocker, causing widespread flooding.

THE BEAUTY OF BUTTERMERE

The next village down the valley is Buttermere, the former home of Mary Robinson, known as the Beauty of Buttermere. Mary became famous in the late eighteenth century as a result of an account given of her by the author of *A Fortnight's Ramble to the Lakes in Westmorland, Lancaster and Cumberland* (1792), see below. Unfortunately, this brought her to the attention of one John Hatfield, a dashing rogue and impostor, who left a trail of unpaid bills and fraudulent transactions wherever he went. John, later known as the Keswick Impostor, proceeded to woo Mary, the innkeeper's daughter at Buttermere, and eventually married her using the assumed name of Alexander Augustus Hope, brother of the Earl of Hopetoun. The wedding took place at Lorton Church on 2 October 1802, the groom having concealed the fact that he already had a wife and two children at Tiverton.

Alas, soon afterwards, his crimes caught up with him. The notice of his wedding in a Scottish newspaper brought his debtors on his trail. He was arrested, arraigned at Carlisle and sentenced to death for forgery. There was widespread public sympathy for his plight but the expected reprieve was not forthcoming and John Hatfield was publicly hanged at The Sands, Carlisle, on Saturday, 3 September 1803. The contemporary newspaper report of this event describes in detail his stoic resignation to his fate and the method of hanging. He stood on a dung cart under the gibbet and the cart was then driven from under him.

Mary, who by this time was expecting a child, eventually got over this experience. She was married to a local statesman of Caldbeck and lived to a ripe old age.

Dramatic as this true-life situation was, the popular press at the time had to embellish it. In about 1841 a novel was published in three volumes for the circulating library, entitled *James Hatfield and the Beauty of Buttermere* by Robert Cruickshank. Apparently this story still has an appeal today. In recent years the Cumbrian author Melvyn Bragg has written a novel around this tale. There follows an extract from a Lakeland guide, first published in 1792, in which the author, Joseph Budsworth, describes his first encounter with the girl who was to become known as the Beauty of Buttermere. In his book Mary is referred to as 'Sally of Buttermere':

> Her mother and she were spinning woollen yarn in the back kitchen; on our going into it, the girl flew away as swift as a mountain sheep, and it was not until our return from Scale Force, that we could say we first saw her; she brought in part of our dinner, and seemed to be about fifteen. Her hair was thick and long, of a dark brown, and though unadorned with ringlets, did not seem to want them; her face was a fine contour, with full eyes, and lips as red as vermillion; her cheeks had more of the lily than the rose and although she had never been out of the village, (and, I hope, will have no ambition to wish it) she had a manner about her which seemed better calculated to set off dress, than dress her. She was a very Lavinia, 'seeming when unadorn'd, adorn'd the most.' When we first saw her at her distaff, after she had got the better of her first fears, she looked an angel, and I doubt not but she is the 'reigning lily' of the valley.
>
> ('A Rambler', 1792)

CRUELTY TO ANIMALS IN THE 1790S

Unfortunately cruelty to our domestic animals is not a new phenomenon. In the book mentioned above, the author describes his visit to Scale Force Waterfall. He recounts that they saw local people hurling dogs over the 172ft fall for 'sport'. He and his party were most disturbed at this and urged the locals to desist. This, thankfully, they did whilst expressing surprise because other visitors had previously enjoyed the spectacle. It was apparently laid on as a spectator sport for visitors. His moving account of how the poor wretched creatures (those that survived the fall) 'limped away looking bewildered at the treatment they had received from their owners', showed a compassion that was sadly lacking in the local Buttermere folk.

Buttermere with inset Scale Force and Mary of Buttermere.

SIR ROWLAND HILL, HIS PENNY POST AND BUTTERMERE

Sir Rowland Hill often visited the Lake District and the story goes that he saw a young woman at a cottage door in Buttermere refuse a letter that the postman had brought. Thinking that she could not afford the high postal rates then prevailing, which were payable on delivery, Sir Rowland spoke to her but was informed that there was no need for his concern. The letter was from her brother, who was working in Penrith, and he and his sister had agreed that, if he was able to come for a holiday at Martinmas, he should put a cross on the right-hand corner of the envelope; if he was unable to do so, the left-hand corner. The cross, the maiden blushingly informed him, was on the right-hand corner, so her brother would be coming at Martinmas, and there was no need for her to open the letter. According to this account, the Buttermere folk were certainly careful with their money. (W.T. McIntyre in the *Cumberland News*, 1939).

However, Morris Danesborough, writing in *Cumbria Magazine*, maintains this story is untrue. Sir Rowland did visit Lakeland in 1823 and kept his family informed of his whereabouts and state of health by a similar method. He is purported to have sent copies of old newspapers to his family, having previously franked the wrappers with the names of MPs (who were allowed to send so many letters free of charge). The postmark indicated the place visited and the name of the MP indicated his state of health. The names of Liberal MPs showed that he was in good fettle, while those of Tory MPs indicated that he was not so well.

The tale of the Buttermere girl originates from an anecdote of Coleridge in *Letters, Conversations and Recollections of S.T. Coleridge.* Coleridge describes passing a cottage near Keswick where a postman was demanding a shilling for a letter: the woman refused to pay and the postman was about to take the letter away when Coleridge paid the fee. The woman told him the letter was from her son and its arrival was sufficient to tell her that he was well. The letter was opened and found to contain a blank sheet of paper. Such frauds were common. Distortion of the story eventually led to the one first described. This was given even more credence when Harriet Martineau, in 1849, published it in her book *A History of England During the Thirty Years' Peace.*

The story was mentioned by Sir Roland Hill in 1837 in a pamphlet on Post Office reform. This eventually led to the introduction of the prepaid penny postage stamp in 1840, for carriage and delivery between any two places in the United Kingdom of Great Britain and Ireland, irrespective of distance.

The tales above give an insight into how local history, through repeated telling, can eventually become myth or legend and an example of this is the valley of Rannerdale, reputed to be the site of the last battle between the Norman conquerors and the local Cumberland people. Rannerdale is famous for its bluebells in the spring, which are known to thrive at the site of a former battle.

In the 1930s Nicholas Size, a local schoolteacher, who lived at the Bridge Hotel, Buttermere, wrote a book called *The Secret Valley* that described how, after the

Norman Conquest, many people unwilling to live under Norman rule fled to the north and the local population, in what is now Cumbria, increased. The main story below is adapted from his book.

The native Cumbrians had already interbred with previous generations of Norse settlers, which might explain a common expression still used today. A common name amongst the Vikings was Storis (now Storey or Story) as common in Norway as Smith is in England. The Storis clan had their family coat of arms, a stork, emblazoned on their shields. So imagine after a few years, when a young Viking warrior has married a local girl and they have a child. When the child asks, 'Where did I come from, Mummy,?' the mother may well have answered, 'The stork brought you dear!'

In about 1070, Boethar the Younger decided to make Buttermere his base from where he could command the defence of Lakeland. It was only much later that the lake and valley became known as Boetharmere or Buttermere. Together with his brother Ackin, Earl Boethar (Jarl in the old Norse, meaning warrior king) set about fortifying their secret valley. They regularly organised attacks on the Norman convoys as they

The Storis crest.

passed up Lonsdale and down the Eden Valley. The local shepherds and farmers would be as fit as our modern fell runners and would know the mountains intimately. They could travel easily and quickly over terrain that would be impossible for the Norman soldiers. As a result, small detachments of Normans would be massacred whenever they ventured away from safety.

The Cumbrians were superior in their archery as well. Their longbow could fire arrows twice as far as the more rapid-firing Norman short bow (which eventually became the crossbow). The increased speed of use of the Norman bow was of little help in guerilla warfare. The Norman soldiers were also superstitious and the small bands of wild men that appeared out of the mountain mists terrified them.

A famous warrior of this time was old Ari Knudson, who devastated many a Norman convoy. He ventured into the wild country between Brough and Alston and organised raids in unexpected places. People to this day still use the phrase 'Fighting like old Harry', so his fame is still not dead after about 900 years.

Ari Knudson.

Eventually the Normans retaliated and this led to three battles in the area, all of which they lost. In the first in the Newlands Valley, west of Derwentwater, the Normans were camped in a very boggy area and the weather was atrocious. In the middle of the night in a downpour of rain they were attacked from above and their camp was set alight. All one of the few survivors could say was: 'A million men or demons had swept over them in the dark and then vanished.'

Incidentally, the Newlands Valley only gained that name many years later when the Monks of Furness owned the land and drained Husaker Tarn near the bottom of the valley and the valley then became arable. To this day the farm in that place is called Uzzicar Farm. A memory of the tarn?

The Normans then amassed a large army at Papcastle, near Cockermouth, and fought their way south towards Crummock Water and Buttermere, resulting in another battle at Brackenthwaite where the locals defended for a time before retreating up Gasgale Gill, to return to Buttermere over the tops. Others evacuated into ships at the head of the lake and these ferried them back to Buttermere.

The Normans, now elated, pressed on, not realising they were being led into a trap. The local people, fearing an eventual attack from the north, had erased all trace of the road over Rannerdale Knotts that led to Buttermere and replaced it with a new road leading into the blind valley of Rannerdale.

The local warriors met with the Normans at earthworks at the entrance to Rannerdale. After a short time they retreated up the hills on both sides and the

Norman cavalry rushed into the valley, following the new road. Horns sounded and a mass of Cumbrian/ Viking warriors, who had been hiding in ships out of sight around the headland, blocked the entrance to the valley. The Normans were then attacked from all sides. Arrows were fired from above, boulders rolled down the slopes and a secret weapon was introduced. Young wild warriors, called 'berserkers', who had drunk liberally of wood alcohol, dressed only in a loincloth and carrying a sword, rushed down the hillsides. They disemboweled the horses, bringing the cavalry men down to the ground. Hence the term, still used today, of 'going berserk'. The Normans were once again routed and there were no further attempts made to conquer the area. Lakeland was at peace until King Stephen, in his attempts to buy friends, ceded it to Scotland, together with Carlisle and the Eden Valley.

AN EARLY MOUNTAIN ACCIDENT

South from Buttermere, at the end of the valley, the road rises up to Honister Pass with its ancient slate mine on the side of Fleetwith Pike. On the lower slopes of Fleetwith, just beyond Gatesgarth Farm, a white cross can be seen at the foot of a crag. This is a memorial to Fanny Mercer, accidentally killed in 1887. Fanny was an 18-year-old servant visiting the lakes with the family of her employer. On the day of the accident Fanny, Walter Clarke, the butler and Clara, another servant, were given the day off and set out for a walk over the fells. They eventually arrived on Honister Crag and decided to return to Buttermere via Fleetwith Pike. It was on their descent, as they neared the road, that the accident happened. Fanny was at the rear, Clara in front and below and Walter Clarke in between. At this point Fanny, taking hold of her alpenstock at the topmost end, leapt from the ledge where she was standing to join Clara. One can only presume that by holding the pole in this manner she thought she was aiding her descent but, instead of sliding her hands down the pole, she clung to the top and the effect was to catapult her right over Walter's head. He caught hold of her dress but failed to stop her and Fanny fell vertically some 20ft, striking her head on a rock and rolling another 100ft or so. She was unconscious and had severe head wounds. Without delay she was taken to Gatesgarth Farm. A mounted messenger was sent the 12 miles to Cockermouth for a doctor, but to no avail. By the time the doctor arrived, about 9 pm, Fanny had died. At the inquest the coroner reported a verdict of 'accidentally killed', saying: 'It was evident the mishap was entirely owing to Miss Mercer not using her alpenstock properly, as otherwise there was no danger at the place where the accident occurred.'

Mountain accidents were less frequent in those times and so a memorial was placed in her memory at the scene of the accident. The inscription reads: 'Friends of Fanny Mercer, accidentally killed 1887.'

2

CARLISLE, THE SOLWAY AND THE NORTH-EASTERN FELLS

CARLISLE

Cumbria's only city, Carlisle, lies to the east of these northern hills. Carlisle originated as a Roman town called Luguvalium. In AD 72/73 a wooden fort was built on the site of the present Tullie House museum extension. It had a turf rampart, two ditches and internal buildings of timber. Another timber fort replaced it around AD 105 and in the late second century the fort was converted to stone, well after the construction of Hadrian's Wall in AD 122.

The Romans left Britain in AD 407 and before long Carlisle, the town, would be abandoned apart from a few farmers living within the walls and farming the land outside. It was the Celts that gave Carlisle its name. They called it Caer Luel, the fortified place belonging to Luel.

From AD 794 Scotland suffered continuous attacks from the Vikings, which extended down into England. By the early tenth century Britain was partitioned into Alba (Scotland) and England. Athelstan of England decided there should only be one ruler and invaded Alba, the start of a 700-year conflict between the two great powers. The Solway to the west of Carlisle became a regular crossing point for invading armies. Edward I of England was remorseless in his attacks on the Scots, gaining the nickname 'Hammer of the Scots' over many years of battle.

In 1307 he returned to the north, intent on fording the Solway at the Sul Wath (wath is the old name for a ford) at Burgh by Sands, 5 miles west of Carlisle. But it was not to be. While preparing for his latest campaign he spent five months at Lanercost Priory as he was in poor health with dysentery, but he did not improve. He made his way to Burgh by Sands, where he rested further but to no avail. He died whilst his attendants were raising him to give him food. A monument to his memory was built by Henry Howard in 1685 which stands to this day on Burgh Marsh.

Old Postcard of King Edward 1 Monument.

More recently, in 2007, a statue to his memory was erected in the village of Burgh. Edward I was an impressive figure for his time, standing 6ft 2in high he was nicknamed Longshanks by his followers. Carlisle owes much to Longshanks. In 1158 the city received its first charter and became an important place because of its strategic position near the Scottish border. In the twelfth century stone walls were built around the town. The Scots occupied the city from 1135 to 1154 and laid siege to Carlisle for three months in 1173, returning in 1315. In both cases they were unable to take the city. As a result of Longshanks and his battles with the Scots, it was more than 300 years before the city was again under siege, this time during the Civil War in 1664. Royalist Carlisle held out against the Roundheads for eight months before surrendering. Isaac Tullie, the 18-year-old son of George Tullie, of Whitehall (later Tullie House), in Abbey Street, Carlisle, wrote a history of the siege, which illustrated how they survived. Here is one example from the book:

Feb. 16, half a score of Scotts Commanders all foxed [intoxicated] came over the water at Etterby [Etterby Wath or ford] and marched as far as ... [Caldew] bridge, where one of them was shot in ye breast and another had his horse shot under him; whereupon the foxt Scotts made a sober retreat. The shot horse was fetched into the town; being a very stately beast, very fat, and because he was not to be cured, Sr Thomas Glenham eat him at his own Table. This was the first horse flesh yt was eaten in the Carlisle siege. This theire bravado was so sudden and unexpected, that very few issued out of ye garrison before they were gone; Cap. Lainyon was one, who making haste to the bridge, tooke a horse from a boy, and charged their leader Capt. Pattin; who finding himselfe wounded, flied towards New Leathes (Newlaithes), which before he could reach, Lanian overtook him, and brought him in, who died the next morning.

The roundheads certainly feared the cavaliers, who made frequent sorties into the countryside for cattle. After the Reformation, Isaac became mayor of Carlisle.

This was not the last siege of Carlisle. In 1745, Bonnie Prince Charlie laid siege to the city for two days before it surrendered. Then in December that year the Duke of Cumberland took back the city after a nine-day siege and bombardment of the castle. The 380 English Jacobite soldiers, of the Manchester regiment, who were garrisoned at the castle were temporarily locked in the cathedral nave before being sent south for trial. Some were returned to be tried at Carlisle, a number being sentenced to be hung, drawn and quartered for treason at Harraby Hill in the city.

Prisoners leaving the castle for execution in 1746.

CARLISLE SHIP CANAL

Few people are aware that Carlisle once had a ship canal linking the city with the Solway at Port Carlisle. In the late eighteenth century Carlisle was lagging behind other towns in the region in that it had no direct access to the sea. The Solway is a very shallow estuary and the nearest approach small ships of 60 to 100 tons could make was Sandsfield jetty about 3½ miles from Carlisle, and then only on a high tide. Goods landed at Sandsfield were then taken by horse and cart into the city. As a result, coal in the city was four times the cost of coal from the pit at Maryport. There were many mills in Carlisle, all powered by water, and it was too expensive to convert to steam, as in other towns that had canals or deep rivers for bulk transport.

Carr's 1836 biscuit works with the canal basin behind.

The canal, completed in 1823, changed all that and Carlisle industry began to boom once more. This was a ship canal similar to the Forth and Clyde canal in Scotland. Ships of up to 120 tons were built at the canal basin in the city. In 1836, George Dixon built the cotton mill in Shaddongate with the famous Dixon's chimney, the largest in Europe at the time, which still towers over the city. At the same time Jonathan Dodgson Carr built his first biscuit factory, which was to become the biggest in the world, next to the canal basin.

PORT CARLISLE

When the canal opened there was nothing at Fishers Cross (now renamed Port Carlisle) except a custom house and a few farms. Within thirty years it had become a small village with a pub, a bowling green, tennis courts and sea water baths. It is now rated as a very special Georgian village as almost all of the buildings are from the same era.

Early in 1830 a news item in the *Carlisle Journal* actually foretold the demise of the canal only seven years after it was built: 'One of Stevenson's locomotive engines intended for the Liverpool and Manchester passed through this town this week, to be shipped at the Canal Basin for Liverpool ... four of Mr Stevenson's locomotives have now been forwarded by our canal.'

By 1836 the first sea-to-sea railway from Newcastle to Carlisle canal basin was completed, soon to be followed by the Maryport to Carlisle railway and, much later, in 1856, by the Lancaster and Caledonian Railway.

Canal closure notice.

The canal was no longer profitable and in 1853, only thirty-two years after being opened, it was drained and within a year the Carlisle to Port Carlisle railway ran along the bed of the canal.

Only two years later a junction was built at Drumburgh, just 1¼ miles from Port Carlisle, and the line was extended to Silloth, which became the new port for Carlisle. Later the railway company decided that the short length of line from Drumburgh to Port Carlisle did not warrant a steam locomotive and it was replaced by two horse-drawn Dandy coaches, one of which can be seen in York Railway Museum. The other was dismantled and the folding side seats are still in use outside the bowling club at Port Carlisle. The port struggled on as a commercial port until 1875, when the Solway Junction Railway viaduct was built across the Solway to take West Cumberland iron ore to Scotland, blocking further shipping.

CARLISLE – THE RAILWAY CITY

The demise of the canal was the direct result of Carlisle becoming the railway city of the north-west of England, which gave a great boost to industry in the city. The textile business of Peter Dixon continued to flourish into the first part of the twentieth century, eventually becoming Todd's Mill. New businesses started up: Cowans Sheldon, crane makers to the world, the Penguin biscuit factory and later, in the 1950s, Kangol, originally hat makers and eventually becoming (very successful) helmet and seat belt manufacturers.

Pirelli tyre makers also came to the city. The Beeching cuts to the railways in the 1960s and the coming of the motorway saw Eddie Stobart build up his iconic transport group. There were, of course, casualties as heavy industry declined and others were moved abroad. Today Carlisle's remaining large employers are McVitie's biscuits, Pirelli tyres and the Stobart Transport Group.

However, one traditional textile factory remains. In 1912 William Linton, originally from Hawick, established his textile factory Linton Tweeds in the old weaving shops at Todd's Mill in Carlisle. By 1928 he had met Coco Chanel and began supplying tweed cloth to her fashion house Chanel Modes. This has continued every year since. This small family firm had its centenary in Carlisle in 2012. It still operates from the same premises in 2017 and continues to supply 'innovative' tweed fabric to Chanel and the rest of the world.

EARLY POLICE FORCE

Carlisle City Police (1827–1967) was one of the earliest police forces in the country, set up to control the lawless behaviour of the residents in the Caldewgate area of the city where the navvies, who had come to build the canal, had settled. Known as the Irish quarter and the Free City, it became notorious and a no-go area for the few watchmen who patrolled at that time.

FIRST BLACK POLICEMAN

More recently it has become known that Carlisle employed Britain's first black policeman, not Birmingham as previously thought. John Kent was appointed to the newly formed Carlisle City Police Force. A black person would have been a rare sight in 1837, so how did this come about?

In the late eighteenth century, Thomas Kent, a black African and a victim of the slave trade, arrived in England from the Caribbean and landed in Whitehaven. He was a servant at Calder Abbey and, after seven or eight years, he went to sea, before returning to Carlisle where he married a Cumbrian girl. They had ten children – one of whom, a son, John, was born at the family home at Low Hesket, Carlisle, sometime between 1795 and 1805. John grew up in the area and married a girl from Longtown. 'In his prime John Kent was a big powerful man,' said the *Carlisle Patriot*, reporting that, at one time he was employed laying pavements in the city and, 'Crowds gathered to watch the tremendous blows dealt with his pavior's beater.' It is clear that the sight of any black person in the city at that time was unusual, let alone a policeman. 'Black Kent's coming' became a household term used to frighten mischievous children into behaving themselves. However, the imputation was ill-deserved. 'Black Kent' in the flesh was a quiet, inoffensive man with a positive fondness for the children who were brought up to regard him as an ogre. Like many in the police at this time, he was eventually fired for drunkenness, which led to a different career as a railway signalman.

John Kent on parade in Carlisle.

His signal box at Carlisle Station became known as Kent's cabin. This is due to the story that the youthful Prince of Wales, when passing through Carlisle on the royal train, shortly after the publication of Harriet Beecher Stowe's book, *Uncle Tom's Cabin*, saw John in his signal box and asked his attendant if that was Uncle Tom in his cabin.

FLOODS IN CARLISLE

Carlisle lies at the confluence of three rivers, the Eden, the Caldew and the Petteril, into which other rivers and streams further up the Eden Valley feed, as can be seen on the map (p.43). This has always caused problems for the city, severe flooding being recorded in the early nineteenth century and the 1930s. However, it was the flooding of Carlisle in 2005 that was unprecedented, arguably the worst ever in the UK at the time. It really hit the headlines and was news around the world. Carlisle's defences were beefed up as a result, £20m being spent to provide the city with (what was described at the time) as protection against a 'once in 200 year event', more severe than in 2005. In fact, this was the best protection anywhere excepting the Thames barrier (proof against a 500-year event).

However, since then, possibly due to global warming, the experts have been proved wrong. Flooding is much more common now than in the past. The 2009 flooding in West Cumbria (Cockermouth, Keswick and Workington in particular) was described as a 1,000-year event. More recently in 2015, Carlisle (along with West Cumbria) suffered more extensive flooding, in spite of the supposed 200-year event protection for the city!

WETHERAL, AND WETHERAL PRIORY

The village of Wetheral, 6 miles to the east of Carlisle is worthy of mention as there is much history there. The Romans quarried the sandstone banks of the River Eden south of the village and ferried the stone downriver to Carlisle to build Stanwix Fort and the Roman wall. One of their officers recorded the fact with inscriptions in the rock (Roman graffiti). 'MAXIMUS SCRIPSIT – LEG XX. V CONDRAUSISIUS', followed by an image of a stag. Translated this reads, 'Maximus wrote this – Condrausisius of the Twentieth legion Valerie Victrix'. Part of this carving fell into the river in 2008 and is now in Tullie House Museum and Art Gallery in Carlisle. The rest is still in situ.

WETHERAL CELLS

These carvings are not far from the Wetheral Cells. They consist of three ancient vaulted rooms carved out of the solid cliff face and are variously known as Wetheral Safeguards, St Constantine's Cells and Constantine's Hermitage. They are very well concealed and may have been used for emergency food storage for the priory above, or the storage of valuables in troubled times. Only the gatehouse of the priory remains. At the dissolution of the monasteries most of the stone went to Carlisle to build the new citadel. The land was given to the diocese of Carlisle and the gatehouse used as a fortified residence for the local vicar.

Near the entrance to the cells is an example of Victorian graffiti. Captain William Mounsey of Castle Street, Carlisle, spent his leisure time carving quotations on rock faces near the Eden. The main text is a verse from the songs of LLywarch Hen, a Welsh poet of the early ninth century. It translates as: 'This leaf which is

Mounsey carving.

being persecuted by the wind, let her beware of her fate: she is old though only born this year.'

Around 1965 the eminent historian Howard Colvin (later knighted) was on a visit to Wetheral when he noticed amongst the rubble of the monuments cleared from the churchyard the sculptured arm of an early cross. Anglo–Saxon lettering was inscribed on the reverse of the stone. Professor Rosemary Cramp dated the stone to the eighth and ninth century. The base of the 1751 sundial in the churchyard is probably the reused socket of this tall cross. It indicates that Christianity had arrived in Wetheral around AD 800, pre-dating the priory and the present church.

As mentioned later in this book, the author Thomas De Quincey, who lived at Dove Cottage, Grasmere, at one time, stayed at his brother Richard's house in 1814 or 1815. The house (now called Eden Croft) is opposite the church entrance. Here he wrote his book *The Stranger's Grave*. The introduction to the book describes the location of the village of Wetheral exactly and the stranger's grave (where itinerants who had been found dead in the parish were buried) is exactly opposite to the upper floor window overlooking the churchyard. Thomas' most famous book was *Confessions of an English Opium Eater*, an autobiography of his life and the effects of his addiction to opium.

The mountainous area, visible to the south-west of Carlisle, called the Caldbeck Fells, are the foothills to two distinct mountains. The nearest of these to the city is Blencathra.

3

THE NORTH-EASTERN FELLS

BLENCATHRA OR SADDLEBACK

The name Blencathra is probably derived from the 'Cumbric' elements *blain* (top, summit) and *cadeir* (seat, chair), meaning 'the summit of the seat-like mountain'. The earlier name of Saddleback is now less well known, probably due to the fact that Alfred Wainwright, of Lakeland guidebook fame, preferred Blencathra.

Cumbric, by the way, is a variety of the common Brittonic language spoken in the Early Middle Ages by inhabitants of this area and southern Scotland.

This fascinating mountain with six separate fell tops guards the north-east corner of the Lake District. Visitors to the area in the eighteenth century often went in fear and awe of the mountains, as shown in this description of an ascent, by four people, by way of Scales Tarn and returning by the aptly named Sharp Edge.

One of the party was 'so astonished with the different appearance of objects in the valley beneath', that he chose to return home. Before they had gone much further another of the four was suddenly taken ill and 'wished to lose blood to calm him down'.

However, he was persuaded to continue to Scales Tarn, where the party, now reduced to three, 'contemplated the scene with awestruck wonder'. Not surprisingly the potential bloodletter refused to continue and was left at the tarn. On returning by way of Sharp Edge the narrator described his impressions as follows:

> We walked back by the side next to the lake, but to look down from thence was so terrible, I could not endure it a moment. We perceived from thence, that my companion, whom we had last left, was laid upon the ground. I pressed the guide to hasten to him, but he refused, alleging that a fog was rising and it would be very hazardous for me to explore my way alone down the mountain. In a short time we were enveloped in a very dense vapour ... the sudden change was incredible. It was with difficulty that we regained the passage, or dry bridge, which we missed on several attempts; and one incautious step would have plunged us into the horrid abyss.

No further mention is made of the hapless bloodletter so it must be presumed they met up with him on the way down. There was obviously a shortage of mountain leadership courses in those days. It goes without saying that you should not abandon people in distress halfway up a mountain.

THE QUARTZ CROSSES ON BLENCATHRA

There are two crosses of white quartz rock set into the ground on the summit plateau between Blencathra and Atkinson Pike. The larger of these was built as a labour of love over many years by Harold Robinson of Threlkeld. Harold, who died in 1988 aged 80, climbed Blencathra sometimes twice a day, each time carrying a stone for the cross. The stone came from the lead mine at Threlkeld, where the Robinsons worked. It was built in memory of Mr Straughan, a great friend of Harold's, who was killed in active service in 1942.

Quartz Cross on Blencathra.

In civilian life Mr Straughan was the gamekeeper at
Skiddaw House. Harold was a dedicated walker and
fell runner. According to his brother, Sid, he preferred
walking to using public transport. He regularly walked
to Maryport and back, some 40 miles. The second
smaller cross was built later by persons unknown using
stones robbed from the larger cross.

GHOST ARMY OF SOUTHER FELL

Stories of ghosts and unexplained visions are plentiful
when one delves into local history. Few, however, are
so well corroborated with dates, times and witness
accounts as the story of the spectre army seen on
Souther Fell (immediately to the east of Blencathra).
Harriet Martineau in her *Guide to the English Lakes* of
1855 gave the most detailed account. Here is a summary
of her tale:

> On Midsummer eve 1735 a farm servant in the employ
> of William Lancaster of Blake Hills Farm, half a mile
> east of Souther Fell, saw the east side of the mountain,
> near the summit, covered with troops, which pursued
> their onward march for over an hour ... When the
> poor fellow told his tale he was insulted on all hands
> ... Two years after, also on Midsummer's eve, Mr
> Lancaster saw some men there, apparently following
> their horses, as if they had returned from hunting.
> He thought nothing of this; but he happened to look
> up again ten minutes after, and saw the figures now
> mounted, and followed by an interminable array of

troops, five abreast, marching from the eminence and over the cleft, as before. All the family saw this, and the manoeuvres of the force as each company was kept in order by a mounted officer galloping this way and that ... Now of course all the Lancasters were insulted, as their servant had been ... On the Midsummer day of the fearful 1745, twenty six persons, expressly summoned by the family, saw all that had been seen before and more ... The witnesses attested the whole story on oath before a magistrate ...

So look for ghosts if you will on Souther Fell, but don't expect anyone to believe you if you see them.

THE IMMORTAL FISH OF BOWSCALE TARN

Mungrisdale valley is bounded by Souther Fell to the south and Bowscale Fell to the north. Bowscale Tarn lies on the northern side of this fell and the path up to it from Mosedale village was a popular Victorian tourist route, probably due to a folk tale dating back several centuries. This tells of two immortal fish that swim in Bowscale Tarn. Wordsworth recalls the tale in his song at the feast of Brougham Castle:

> Both the undying fish that swim
> in Bowscale Tarn did wait on him;
> The pair were servants of his eye
> In their immortality;
> They moved about in open sight,
> To and fro for his delight

CALDBECK COMMON AND
ITS MINING LEGACY

The low rolling fells to the north of Blencathra were a hive of activity in former years; lead, copper, zinc, and more recently (in the first part of the twentieth century) barytes and tungsten were mined here. When one walks along the track from Fellside Farm towards Roughtengill evidence of this is all around, with water hush marks from earlier times and spoil heaps from the nineteenth century dotted around the hillsides.

Queen Elizabeth I is said to have called these fells her treasure chest. The most strategic metal at the time was copper, which was used to copper bottom her fighting ships, thus keeping them barnacle-free and faster in the water than those of the Spanish Armada.

The remains of a lead smelter can be seen along this route with the marks left by the smelter chimney on Hay Knott that was laid up the side of the hill. Lead oxide in the fumes from the smelting would condense inside this long chimney, and every so often workers would have to climb up it to retrieve the white lead oxide while breathing in the fine powder. Hence their average life expectancy was about thirty years.

It is hard to imagine that more than 150 years ago this valley provided work for more than 100 miners. The lead was needed for plumbing and roofing in the new cities of the industrial revolution and most of the lead ore contained up to 8 per cent silver, which was often worth more than the lead.

In the twentieth century many thousands of tons of barytes were mined in the Sandbeds area of these

Hay Knott from Brae Fell - showing the marks left by the smelter chimney.

fells, providing barium oxide for the chemical and pharmaceutical industry. A less well-known use for barium at this time was as an additive to concrete used as an absorptive shield against gamma and X-radiation in the emerging nuclear industry. The mines finally closed in the early 1960s.

The other large mountain in the Caldbeck area, visible from Carlisle, is Skiddaw.

SKIDDAW

At 3,054ft (931m) Skiddaw is one of only three English mountains more than 3,000ft high, all of which are in the Lake District, and are sometimes referred to as the English Munros. The lower slopes of Skiddaw were probably a hunting ground for the Norse settlers of the ninth and tenth centuries and they gave the mountain the name Skytja-haugr, shooters hill. Written evidence supports this as the name was recorded as Skithoc in 1231 and Skythouc a little later. In fact the eastern slopes of the mountain, down as far as Skiddaw House, eventually became known as Skiddaw Forest.

Ullock Pike ridge route to Skiddaw.

D. LUSH.

An easily accessible mountain, Skiddaw, with its broad, rounded summit, was an important beacon station in years gone by with two beacons to be maintained. It was Macaulay in the last century who wrote a patriotic poem that described how the news of the sighting of the Spanish Armada was passed from beacon to beacon until the whole country was warned. The last two lines read as follows:

Til Skiddaw saw the fire that burned on Gaunt's embattled pile,
    And the red glare from Skiddaw roused the burghers of Carlisle.

Now research indicates that 'Gaunt's embattled pile' is the hill in the middle of Lancaster. It is most unlikely that a beacon in Lancaster could have been seen from Skiddaw and much more likely that the message followed the coast from Lancaster to Beacon Hill, Barrow then on to Workington by Black Combe, Muncaster, Boothill and St Bees Head. The glow from Workington across the Solway Plain would be the signal to put the torch to Skiddaw's two beacons.

A more recent bonfire on Skiddaw was in celebration of the Queen's Jubilee in 1977. Unfortunately the author can vouch for the fact that the burghers of Carlisle never saw that glow, neither did the people of Keswick. The 500 people or so on the summit that night, including the narrator, had difficulty seeing the fire from more than 50 yards distant. The July weather was foul, with driving rain and sleet. That night will be remembered for a long time, not least for the fact that, whilst leading a party on the descent towards Dash Farm, in complete darkness, the party strayed from their compass bearing and ended up over Dead Crags. The author's friends lost no time in pointing out to him that the fell on which this occurred was called 'Cockup' and just across the way, beyond the crags, was 'Great Cockup'.

THE GIANT OF THE BROCKEN

The summit of Skiddaw is one of the few mountains in the Lake District where cloud conditions occasionally arise such that one can observe a Brocken Spectre, so named as the phenomenon was first recorded as being seen on Mount Brocken in the Harz Mountains in

Image of Brocken Spectre seen on Skiddaw.

Germany. They are best seen when the sun is low in the sky and casts your shadow on to cloud or mist lying below you. A rainbow-coloured halo is seen around the shadow.

SKIDDAW HOUSE

The Back o' Skiddaw is the area to the east of the summit that descends to Glenderaterra Beck. There, in an isolated grove of trees to the north-east of Sale How, is Skiddaw House, an unexpected sight in such a remote terrain. Originally built around 1830 by Lord Lonsdale for his gamekeepers and shepherds, it is now a youth hostel, ideally situated for those walking the Cumbrian Way. The section from Keswick rises up onto Latrigg and follows the old sled route that traverses around Lonscale Crags, with its old slate workings, towards Skiddaw House. Remains of the old shielings and drystone huts, built by the slate workers long ago, are still to be seen. The gently graded sled route would be used to transport slate and stone from Lonscale quarries to build Crosthwaite Church and other buildings in Keswick from the twelfth century onwards.

According to John Martin in his book *The Loneliest House in England,* Pearson Dalton, a local shepherd, arrived at Skiddaw House in 1922. Until the last married shepherd left in 1957 there was always a resident shepherd and his family, as well as, as often as not, a resident gamekeeper with or without a family. After 1957, for at least the next twelve years, Pearson lived alone at the house from Monday to Friday. Later the

Skiddaw House.

house was abandoned for a time. Then a group called
Border Bothies used the east end as a mountain bothy. In
the late 1960s when comprehensive education came to
Carlisle, a group of teachers, disaffected with the system
change, set up a private school in Fisher Street, Carlisle,
called Overwater School. The school only survived until
1978 but during that time they restored the west end of
Skiddaw House as a field centre for their students. Later,
due to lack of maintenance and planning problems it
was abandoned. The YHA operated the building as
a simple hostel from about 1990 until 2002, when it
closed. The house was reopened in April 2007 as an
independent hostel. The old YHA Friends of Skiddaw
House group was re-formed as Skiddaw House
Foundation, a registered charity, with the declared aim
of maintaining the house as a hostel in the long term
whilst retaining the principles of the YHA. Skiddaw
House is once more welcoming visitors.

PROPOSED DAMMING OF MOSEDALE AND MUNGRISDALE

Skiddaw House overlooks Mosedale to the north, the source of the River Caldew. Few people know that in the water resources review in the 1950s it was suggested that a dam be built in Mosedale to create a reservoir backing up almost to Skiddaw House. It was even suggested that a dam be built in Mungrisdale, above the village, to give a supply of up to 5 million gallons a day. There were four plans put forward for dams in Mosedale that could supply water to Penrith, Wigton and Cockermouth rural districts.

Luckily however, unlike the damming of Thirlmere and Haweswater in the first half of the twentieth century, the proposal was thrown out and the view down Mosedale from Skiddaw House is unchanged.

Walkers continuing north along the Cumbria Way long-distance path from Skiddaw House via Mosedale, are travelling along the bed of the formerly proposed reservoirs until they reach the junction of Grainsgill Beck, where a left turn is made up on to Little Lingy Fell. The abandoned mine at this junction was one of the last working mines in the area. Carrock tungsten mine is the only one outside of Cornwall at which wolfram (an oxide of tungsten) has been mined in this country. Changes in the price of tungsten over the years caused it to be put on a care and maintenance basis several times.

Tungsten was mined here in the years leading up to the First World War in the form of wolframite and sheelite. It was used in the production of munitions and ironically the mine was managed by two Germans.

The mine reopened in 1977 when 16,000 tonnes per annum of wolfram were being produced until final closure in 1981. The site was cleared in 1988 and bulldozed as close to the original contours as possible. The only remains of buildings left on the site are those on the south side of Grainsgill Beck, the concrete bases of hoppers constructed in 1913 by the Carrock Mining Syndicate.

Continuing on to Little Lingy and then Great Lingy Fell, a hut is encountered, looking like the chicken crees or huts of the 1950s. This is Lingy Hut with a book to sign for travellers and where one can stay overnight on a raised wooden platform inside. When taking Duke of Edinburgh Scheme students on practice walks in the Caldbecks in March, often in snow, the author and colleagues would keep up their spirits by telling them that they could lunch at Lingy Hut, where there was a café. Imagine their faces when they saw the real thing!

The Cumbria Way continues on northwards towards High Pike. The ridge seen leading off to the east rises to the top of Carrock Fell. This is the site of the largest and most strategically placed Iron Age fort in the district.

Remains of other forts are to be seen at Castle Howe, Peel Wyke on Bassenthwaite, at Dunmallet on Ullswater,

Carrock Fort.

at Mardale Castle Crag, at Borrowdale Castle Crag and at Reecastle Crag above Lodore Beck in Borrowdale. Prior to the Roman invasion, Cumbria was ruled by the Brigantes and Carrock Fort was possibly the capital of this tribe. The artist's impression on page 64 is from a guide book published in the early nineteenth century when, presumably, the remains were more upstanding than they are today.

Skiddaw overlooks Keswick and Borrowdale to the south. The town of Keswick is now, of course, a holiday resort, less spoilt than the more commercial area of the Lake District such as Bowness-on-Windermere. Known for its incredible number of outdoor shops, Keswick is a magnet for walkers, climbers and cyclists as well as general holidaymakers.

4

KESWICK AND BORROWDALE

KESWICK

The name is probably from the old English meaning 'farm where cheese is made', the word deriving from *cēse* (cheese), with a Scandinavian initial 'k', and *wīc* (special place or dwelling). The name first appeared in writing about 1234 relating to the purchase of land by William de Derwentwater from the monks of Furness Abbey. Part of the deal gave the monks 'lea ye to ha ye a mill dam on William's land of Kesewic'. This is simply Kesewic, or the cheese dairy of the Derwentwater estate. So Keswick originated from a cheese farm near Crosthwaite.

KESWICK CONVENTION

The town hosts the Keswick Convention, which began in 1875. It was founded by Anglican canon T.D. Harford-Battersby, and Quaker Robert Wilson. They held the first Keswick Convention in a tent on the lawn of St John's vicarage, Keswick, beginning with a prayer meeting on the evening of Monday, 28 June. During the conference (which continued until Friday morning) more than 400 people attended, uniting under the banner of 'All One in Christ Jesus', which is still the convention's watchword. The convention has increased in size and organisation ever since, so that now upwards of 3,000 people attend during the three-week event. In 2015, Keswick Ministries bought the redundant Keswick pencil factory building. The director of Keswick Ministries, James Robson, described the refurbishment of this site as a project that will serve 'the next generation – a project about people'. The aim is to 'unify the site' by offering a central space in which all activities take place, with a new marquee being built that will accommodate 4,000 people.

THEATRE BY THE LAKE

The Blue Box was an extraordinary mobile theatre created after the Second World War to take plays to towns and cities with no active theatres. It was a regular visitor to Keswick with its long convoy of wagons, including dressing rooms, bedsits and canteen, grinding up and down the Lake District hills. The Blue Box settled permanently in a car park in Keswick in 1975 and retired to Snibston Discovery Park in Leicestershire in 1996.

The present Theatre by the Lake opened on the shores of Derwentwater in August 1999 as a permanent replacement for the Blue Box. It was the last theatre to be built in Britain in the old millennium and the first to be built with the help of money from the National Lottery. It has since staged more than 100 plays, commissioned new work, established a reputation for high production values and found a loyal all-year-round audience in the people of Cumbria and visitors to the Lake District.

CASTLERIGG STONE CIRCLE

Castlerigg Stone Circle lies about a mile to the east of Keswick. It is perhaps the most atmospheric and dramatically sited of all British stone circles, with panoramic views towards the mountains of Helvellyn and High Seat. It is also among the earliest British circles, raised in about 3000 BC during the Neolithic period. Taken into guardianship in 1883, it was also one of the first monuments in the country to be recommended for preservation by the state.

Most stone circles are Bronze Age burial monuments (dating from approximately 2,000–800 BC) containing cremations in central pits or beneath small central cairns. However, their Neolithic forebears, such as Castlerigg, Swinside in the southern part of the Lake District, and Long Meg and her Daughters in the Eden Valley, do not contain formal burials. One of the more unusual features of Castlerigg is a rectangle of standing stones within the circle; there is only one other comparable example, at the Cockpit, an open stone circle at Askham Fell, above Ullswater.

Druidical Circle near Keswick in Cumberland.

Castlerigg Stone Circle in 1783.

THE GREAT DEED OF BORROWDALE

The manor of Barrowdale (Dale of the Castle) had been granted to the monks of Furness Abbey by the Derwentwater family. At the dissolution of the monasteries the property reverted to the Crown and was later sold by James I to two Londoners. For reasons unknown, these two worthies promptly sold the estate to the tenants for less than a single year's revenue and the contract for this sale, dated 1613, became known as the Great Deed of Borrowdale.

The folk of Cumberland and Westmorland (Cumbria) generally used to think of the Borrowdale people as rather simple and unsophisticated. In the same way that an Englishman tells jokes about the Irish, or a German tells jokes about the Swiss, so the burghers of Keswick told tales about the inhabitants of Borrowdale. These were recorded in 1855 by author and traveller Harriet Martineau:

> It is said that an old Borrowdale Man was once sent a very long way for something very new, by some innovator who had found his way into the dale. The man was to go with horse and sacks (for there were no carts, because there was no road) to bring some lime from beyond Keswick. On his return, when he was near Grange, it began to rain; and the man was alarmed at seeing his sacks begin to smoke. He got a hatful of water from the river; but the smoke grew worse. Assured at length that the devil must be in any fire that was aggravated by water, he tossed the whole load into the river.

That must have been before the dalesmen built their curious wall; for they must have had lime for that. Spring being very charming in Borrowdale, and the sound of the cuckoo gladsome, the people determined to build a wall to keep in the cuckoo, and make the spring last forever. So they built a wall across the entrance, at Grange. The plan did not answer; but that was, according to the popular belief from generation to generation, because the wall was not built one course higher. It is simply for want of a top course in that wall that eternal spring does not reign in Borrowdale.

Another anecdote shows, however, that a bright wit did occasionally show himself among them:

A 'statesman' [an 'estateman; or small proprietor] went one day to a distant fair or sale and brought home what neither he nor his neighbours had ever seen before; a pair of stirrups. Home he came jogging, with his feet in his stirrups; but by the time he reached his own door, he had jammed his feet in so fast that they would not come out. There was great alarm and lamentation but, as it could not be helped now, the good man patiently sat his horse in the pasture for a day or two, his family bringing him food, till the eldest son, vexed to see the horse suffering by exposure, proposed to bring both into the stable. This was done; and there sat the farmer for several days, his food being brought to him as before. At length, it struck the second son that it was a pity not to make his father useful, and release the horse; so he proposed to carry him, on the saddle, into the house. By immense exertion it was done; the horse being taken alongside the midden in the yard, to ease the fall: and the good man found himself under his own roof again, spinning wool in a corner of the kitchen. There the mounted man sat spinning, through the cleverness of his second son, till the lucky hour arrived of his youngest son's return, he being a scholar, a learned student from St Bees. After duly considering the case, he gave his counsel. He suggested that the good man should draw his feet out of his shoes. This was done, amidst the blessings of the family; and the good man was restored to his occupations and to liberty. The wife was so delighted that she said if she had a score of children, she would make them all scholars, if only she had to begin life again.

WEATHER LORE – THE BORROWDALE SOP

The Borrowdale Sop.

The Borrowdale Sop is a small cloud that rises at times at the Head of Borrowdale, near Piers Ghyll. Gradually growing larger, it floats away down the Derwent valley over Styhead Tarn. If it goes over towards the Vale of St John the weather will continue to be fine, but if it takes the direction of Langdale, rain will follow within the next twenty-four hours.

GOLDSCOPE MINE

German ore miners came to Cumberland in 1564 from Augsburg in Germany to mine strategic metals, copper, lead, silver and gold for Queen Elizabeth I. She was concerned in those warlike times not to be dependent on foreign supplies of copper, silver and gold in particular. England had no previous experience of deep mining but the Germans were recognised as experts in this field. The mine under Hindscarth became known as Gottes Gab ('God's gift' in German), which over the years changed to Goldscope.

Many of Cumbria's landed gentry were originally German in origin. Indeed, many well-known surnames in the county such as the Tullies of Carlisle, the Banks of Keswick, the Nicholsons of Hawkshead Hall and the Rawlinsons of Grisedale originated in these early unions between the German miners and local families. Other names still to be found in the area are Senogles and Stamper (Stampfer).

Castle Crag with Derwentwater beyond.

CASTLE CRAG

Castle Crag is the central 'tonsil' of the jaws of Borrowdale. A thousand years ago it was occupied as a hill fort by Norman invaders who were trying to control the local inhabitants, unsuccessfully as it turned out. In the eighteenth and nineteenth century it was a slate quarry, which explains its present state with open workings, stacks of slate and several large caves, from which the better slate was extracted.

However, Castle Crag is best known for its resident hermit in the early part of the twentieth century.

THE HERMIT OF CASTLE CRAG

Millican Dalton was born at Nenthead near Alston in 1867. He worked at a shipping office in London until the age of 30 and over the years he became a lover of the simple life. He became an early refugee from the rat race when he gave up his job to become a professional camper and guide, leading organised tours in the Lake District, Scotland and Switzerland. When in England he spent his time between Epping Forest and the Lake District, spending three months every summer in a man-made cave on the east side of Castle Crag. He soon became quite famous as 'the Professor of Adventure' and would give instruction in the art of

Carving on the entrance to 'Attic'.

raft building, sailing and rock climbing. Millican was a colourful character. He made his own clothes and equipment, wore shorts, a slouch hat with pheasant feather and a tweed coat. He was a strict vegetarian and a Quaker. Millican finally died in 1947 at the age of 80. One memorial to him still exists; one that was wrought by his own hand. At the entrance to the upper cave, his sleeping quarters known as the Attic, one can still see the carving on the wall of his favourite saying, 'Don't Waste Words ... Jump to Conclusions!'

Millican Dalton was not the only hermit who became well known in the area. Skiddaw can boast a hermit as well. About 1864 a Scotsman from Banffshire, one George Smith, came to the mountain and built himself a hut on a ledge of Skiddaw Dodd, now covered by Dodd Wood (not far from where the osprey nest is today). McIntyre described how George, in order to enter his lair, had to climb a wall and then drop down through a hole into the interior of the dwelling. His table was a stone and he slept on a bed of leaves. He wore no hat, coat or shoes, washed his single shirt in the water of the beck and let it dry upon his back. He frequently ate his meals uncooked and was so partial to whisky that he sometimes found himself in the hands of the police. His ostensible means of livelihood was the painting of portraits, but as he often refused payments for these, his survival was somewhat of a mystery. Alas his home was eventually destroyed by the nineteenth-century version of our 'yobs' and George went to live in Keswick. He suffered from religious mania, however, and was finally removed to an asylum in his native Banffshire, where he most probably died.

BARROWDALE WELL

In a field at Manesty, adjacent to the minor road from
Grange to Portinscale, is Barrowdale Well, marked
Salt well on the OS map. The well is surrounded by
a rectangular stone wall with steps descending down
into the water. According to Thomas Short in his 'Essay
towards a Natural, Experimental and Medicinal History
of the Mineral Waters of England' published in 1740,
'it was first found by miners, digging in their quest for
ore'. These would be the German miners who arrived in
1564. He goes on to compare it with water from other
spas or wells. See below.

The Natural H I S T O R Y.   85

Hiftory *Of Purging Waters from Marine Salt only.*

I T's not an account of all thofe Waters in this large diftrict we in-
tend, this would lead to give a Hiftory of the Brine Pits, *Wiches*
and *Salt works*, but thefe not being reckoned Medicinal mineral
Waters, I fhall give a few of thofe reputed and ufed as fuch and firft.

Barrowdale Well, near *Grange*, three Miles from *Kefwick* in
Cumberland, it lies in a Level near a Mofs; it was found at firft by
Miners digging in Queft of Ore, and fprings out of the hard blew-
ftone which conftitutes all thofe awfull Mountains, and terrible precipices called *Fells*. being a kind of *Lapis fciffilis*, is pretty folid
of a blewifh Colour, and much of it will bear a pretty good Glofs
in polifhing. It's a rough, fevere purge to ftrong Conftitutions,

A small section of the 'Essay'.

THE BOWDER STONE

Venturing further into Borrowdale along the road towards Rosthwaite is a parking area for the Bowder Stone on the left side of the road. A short walk through the woods to the east brings one to this curiosity, described as early as 1749 as the largest stone in England. The land around the Bowder Stone was bought in 1798 by Joseph Pocklington, who made the stone a tourist attraction. He built the cottage at the end of the eighteenth century within a stone's throw of the Bowderstone rock, 'for an old woman to live in who is to show the rock, for fear travellers should pass under it without seeing it'. Pocklington was the first to provide a ladder to climb to the top. The stone is actually called the Balder* stone. On one side there is the face of Balder and a small hole was said to exist where an arrow enters Balder's head. There appears to be a second face on the stone, just behind the face of Balder. The face is flatter but still recognisable as a face.

The two faces of 'Balder'.

Altogether there were four families who lived there over the years: the Carradus, the Thompsons, the Weightmans and the Peppers. Bowderstone Cottage today is owned by the National Trust and is a climbing hut for the Northumbrian Mountaineering Club. Dr Alan Smith debates in detail in his book how the stone came to be in its present position. He concludes, after considering various possibilities, that the overwhelming evidence is that the stone fell from Bowder Crag between 13,500 and 10,000 years ago.

* In Lower Saxony in the forest of Mailburg in the county of Osnabrücke there is a pagan cult stone known as the Pfaohlenstein. Its name derives from the Germanic God Pfaohi, Balder, son of Woden (Odin). Perhaps the name "Bowderstone" derives from "Balder" and the stone was named by the German miners who came to Borrowdale in 1564 to mine copper.

DERWENTWATER

Derwentwater is a shallow lake compared to the rest of the major lakes in Cumbria. This became very clear to the author when out on the lake in canoes with schoolchildren near the activity centre in Lingholm woods. The group were at least 100m from the shore when the author, as a teacher supervising the children, accidentally rolled his canoe and fell out. Imagine his surprise when, treading water, he realised he was touching the bottom. When he stood up the water was about level with his waist. As a result the southern end of the lake is a 'moveable feast' depending on the weather. Sometimes the public footpath from Lodore in the east to Manesty in the west can be used, at other times it is under water.

Derwentwater has four permanent islands and one 'floating' island (reputedly) that sporadically appears towards the end of summer and consists of a mass of vegetable matter that rises to the surface on a cushion of methane gas!

Lords Island on the lake has an interesting history. In the sixteenth century there was a smelter on the island to process the lead ore from the surrounding mines. This was probably because of the value of the refined ore, particularly the silver content of the lead. Having the smelter on the island would help with security. Unfortunately during the Civil War the smelter was destroyed and the miners either killed or conscripted into the Parliamentary army. The smelter was fuelled by wood from the surrounding hills and the treeless landscape today on Causey Pike and other local hills dates from that time. However, remains of the original oak forest can still be seen on the south side of the Causey Pike ridge.

ROSTHWAITE IN BORROWDALE

Rosthwaite is famous for its association with the author Hugh Walpole. As a gay man at a time when homosexual practices were illegal for men in Britain, Walpole conducted a succession of intense but discreet relationships with other men, and was for much of his life in search of what he saw as 'the perfect friend'. He eventually found one, a married policeman, with whom he settled in the Lake District. Walpole's output was large and varied. He wrote thirty-six novels between 1909 and 1941, but he is probably best known for his *Herries Chronicle* series of novels. In 1930 Walpole wrote *Rogue Herries*, an historical novel set in Borrowdale. He followed it with three sequels; all four novels were published in a single volume as *The Herries Chronicle*. Rogue Herries' fictional home in the novels is widely recognised to be Hazel Bank (now a guest house), just above the village on the track leading over to Watendlath. His novels tell of life in the area in the eighteenth century.

WATENDLATH AND WATENDLATH TARN

In days gone by the hamlet of Watendlath, in a high valley above Rosthwaite, at 263m above sea level, was a very busy place. It was an important staging post for the packhorse drivers of old as several routes cross here. The name Watendlath describes well its situation, stemming from the Norse *Vaten Lath* or Lake farm buildings. Nowadays there are tea rooms at the farm. It is a car tourist hotspot for those willing to tackle the long, twisty and narrow road from the Borrowdale Road at Ashness Bridge.

Walkers, of course, use the shorter track from Rosthwaite. For those on foot another tarn worth visiting, particularly in July and August, is Dock Tarn.

This is done by crossing the packhorse bridge and following the path along the western edge of Watendlath Tarn. Dock Tarn is completely covered by water lilies in the summer months. This must have been the case for at least 1,000 years, as the name can be traced back to its Anglo–Saxon origins as *dockerterne*, 'the lily covered lake' (*docce* – plant that swims).

Watendlath's packhorse bridge is probably the most photographed of its type in England. A little known fact is that in 2015 the bridge was named fourth best bridge in England on which to play Poohsticks.

AULD JWONNY HOOSE, LANGSTRATH BLOOMERY AND EAGLE CRAG

An old packhorse route leads east from Stonethwaite up and over Greenup Edge, eventually dropping down into Grasmere. A mile or so from Stonethwaite, a long valley joins from the south, Langstrath (Old Norse – Long Valley) where Langstrath Beck joins Greenup Gill.

The ruined old building near the end of this valley was once an inn known as Auld Jwonny Hoose. Johnny ran the inn about the beginning of the nineteenth century and would catch the trade from both packhorse routes. Further along Langstrath on the left is the site of an old bloomery. The iron smelter was sited here to use the local forest for fuel, leaving the hills today as open fellside, as at Causey Pike. Iron ore would be brought through Ure Gap (Ore Gap) between Esk Pike and Bowfell and over Stake Pass from the mines in Eskdale (before the railway came to Eskdale).

Eagle Crag stands near the corner of these two valleys. There are many Eagle Crags in the dales as the birds were quite common in the past. Among these Eagle Crags is the one above Thirlmere, another between Patterdale and Grisedale Hause and, best known of all, the fine rock in Borrowdale on the way to Greenup Edge. This Eagle Crag was one of their last haunts and the last eagle was shot here over 200 years ago. In the eyes of the local farmers they were a menace as they took lambs, hare, partridge and grouse in abundance. In 1769, the poet Gray described how the local farmers in Borrowdale controlled the birds:

> He was let down from the cliff in ropes to a shelf of rock, on which the nest was built, the people above shouting and hollowing [*sic*] to fright the old birds, which flew screaming round but did not dare to attack him. He brought off the eaglet for there is seldom more than one. ... Seldom a year passes but they take the brood or eggs, and sometimes they shoot one.

Eagles continued to nest in the valley for another fourteen years until the last one was shot and eagles no longer survived in England. However, in more recent times (1970) a pair returned, probably from the south of Scotland, to nest in Riggindale above Haweswater.

CUMBERLAND PENCIL COMPANY
AND THE WAD MINES AT SEATOLLER

At the southern end of Borrowdale is Seathwaite, famous as the wettest place in England, according to meteorological records. Above Seathwaite Farm on Seatoller Fell are the ancient wad mines (pronounced wod) where the pipes of graphite (or wad) were mined from the 1550s. In the early days the wad was used for sheep marking and rust-proofing stoves (black leading). However, it was mainly used to construct crucibles and refractory moulds when dealing with molten metals.

Pencil making in 1850.

A later use was that of pencil leads. Keswick was the home of the first pencil and the first pencil factory. Previously the pencils had been made by hand in small workshops, but in 1832 Bankes, Son & Co. opened a factory in the town.

This company would pass through several hands before becoming the Cumberland Pencil Company in 1916. Although pencils are no longer produced in Keswick there is a pencil museum that tells the story of the wad mines at Seathwaite. The price of graphite fluctuated greatly over the years from £18 a ton in 1646 to £3,920 a ton in 1804. As a result, pilfering and illicit working was a problem. Miners were undressed and inspected internally on leaving the mine and armed guards were employed to prevent people raking over the spoil heaps.

John Adams, in his book on *Mines of the Lake District Fells*, describes how one example of illicit working was solved:

In 1749 a particularly crafty attempt was made to work the mine illicitly by a man called William Hetherington. He obtained a lease to drive a copper adit on the site and actually found some copper. However, as the working contained a secret door giving access to the wad mine, Hetherington and friends did quite well for a while. On discovering what was happening the Bankes family cleverly solved the problem by appointing Hetherington as steward – set a thief to catch a thief!

Stealing wad was such a problem that in 1752, after an armed attack on the mine, an Act of Parliament was passed making it a felony to illegally enter or steal wad from a mine. The punishment was a public whipping plus one year's hard labour, or seven years' transportation.

West of this mountainous area of Cumbria are the coastal towns that, in the past and to a certain lesser extent today, were the industrial centres of the county. In the north-west corner is Silloth, actually the youngest town in the area.

5

THE COASTAL TOWNS OF CUMBRIA

SILLOTH AND SKINBURNESS

The name Silloth originated from Sea-lath, meaning the barn by the sea. It was part of the Grange farm of Holme Cultram Abbey. Skinburness, a hamlet a couple of miles north, was the centre of population in earlier times. The name is thought to mean 'the headland of the demon-haunted castle'. The headland is Grune Point. In 1299, Edward I gathered a fleet for the invasion of Scotland at the port of Skin Burness. With about fifty ships he sheltered in the lee of the point waiting for his moment to come and seize the land around the Solway for England from the Scots, led by Wallace. He later granted the town of 'skimmed the nest' charters for a market and fair. The charters referred to Skinburness rather than Silloth, as Silloth was a small hamlet with little population at that time. The present town of Silloth only developed after the arrival of the railway in 1854, very quickly outgrowing Skinburness. A more recent royal connection is when King George I planned to visit Silloth (in favour of Bognor Regis) for its healthy air to overcome his illness. Elaborate plans were drawn up to alter the town as a result of an impending visit by the king. However, they never came to fruition as the king was too ill to travel so far north.

When the Carlisle Canal closed in 1853 to be replaced by a railway, a junction was built at Drumburgh to take the railway to Silloth, then only a hamlet. Within a few years the Marshall dock was built and Carrs built a flour mill there. Silloth then became the new port for Carlisle and is one of only two working ports left on the Solway. To this day boats registered at Silloth start with the letters CL in their registration as Carlisle canal basin was the original port for Carlisle.

Within a short time Silloth became a holiday resort and expanded with thousands of day trippers coming to the coast from Carlisle. On 4 August 1911, 4,297 people travelled to Silloth by rail. This broke the

OPENING OF THE MARSHALL DOCK AT THE PORT OF SILLOTH

Opening of the Marshall dock in 1859.

previous record set on Whit Monday 1906 when 3,944 made the journey. Silloth became an annual holiday destination for visitors from southern Scotland and this still continues to this day.

The Second World War changed the look of this little corner of England forever. Three large airfields were built – at Silloth, Kirkbride and, further north, at Anthorn. Their runways and many of the buildings remain – as much a part of the landscape as the farms and the sea banks. Silloth was planned as a maintenance and training centre, the site being chosen because of its remoteness from what were expected to be the main operational airfields further south. In 1939, the No. 1 Operational Training Unit of Coastal Command was established there. Its job was to train bomber crews and the Lockheed Hudson was the plane chiefly used for this work. During the early years of the war, there was an alarmingly high casualty rate amongst them. By the end of 1942, seventeen Hudsons and one Oxford bomber trainer had crashed; three more were lost at sea. Fifty-six members of their crews are buried at Causewayhead, and many more bodies were never recovered. To this day the Solway off Silloth is still called Hudson Bay by the locals, due to the large number of young pilots lost there, many from Commonwealth countries.

The movie *A Yank in the RAF* came out in 1941, some months before America entered the war. Tyrone Power plays an American pilot who gets a job ferrying bombers from Canada to England. In London, he meets an old flame, Betty Gable, who is working as a showgirl in the West End. He joins the RAF to impress her and

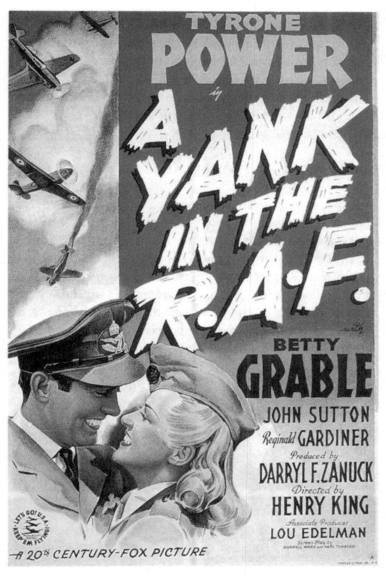

Poster 'Yank in the RAF'.

becomes a bomber pilot. Later, he is transferred to a fighter squadron and takes part in the evacuation of Allied troops from Dunkirk.

Many of the flying sequences were filmed at Silloth, although the contributions of the big Hollywood stars were obviously filmed in the studios there.

ALLONBY

Further down the coast is Allonby, a coastal village that still retains much of its original character. Allonby has a long sandy beach, with fine views across the Solway Estuary to the mountains of southern Scotland. The Cumbrian Coastal Way passes through the village, and walkers can enjoy many miles of sand dunes. At the beginning of the twentieth century Allonby was the home of a surprising business – ship dismantling. At the south end of the village, the Twentyman family operated a ship-breaking business. John Twentyman, a

Ship hulls to be broken up at Allonb.

retired mariner, started this in the 1880s, but business peaked in the early 1900s as steel replaced wood in the construction of new vessels. Several local men and boys were employed there. The wood was salvaged for use by local builders.

There was great excitement in the village in 1903 when the barque *Hougoumont* ran aground there. No lives were lost but part of the ship's cargo was scattered all over the shore. The villagers mounted a 'salvage operation'. The crates contained tins of salmon, peaches and pears but were unlabelled. The only way to tell which was which was by shaking them; if the contents moved, it was fruit. A good time, and a few good meals, were had by all. This was at a time when there was much poverty in the area. Echoes of *Whisky Galore*?

The next village to the south along the coast was called Ellenfoot in the eighteenth century, as it is situated at the mouth of the River Ellen. At that time it was described as 'the resort of a few miserable fishermen who had a few huts along the beach'.

Locals salvaging the cargo washed up at Allonby in 1903.

MARYPORT

That all changed within a few years as, in 1749, an Act of Parliament was passed to allow the creation of the present town. Humphrey Senhouse named the new town after his wife, Mary. The Senhouse family were landowners in the area and responsible for the development of the town and excavation of its Roman past. Maryport then developed along the lines of Whitehaven before it, becoming an industrial centre. An iron foundry opened and the port developed, as did shipyards such as Wood's yard and Ritson's yard, which was famous for launching ships broadside into the River Ellen. By this time, coal mines were operating all around the town – at Ellenborough, Dearham, Gilcrux, Broughton Moor and Birkby. A large coal trade developed exporting to Ireland, where peat was the main available fuel. At the turn of the nineteenth century steel railway lines from the steelworks at Workington were exported all over the world from Maryport. This boom time came to an end in 1927 when a new deep-water dock was opened in Workington and the import of iron ore and export of finished steel products was transferred there. Now Maryport is a tourist town but it still has some fishing boats and a marina for pleasure craft.

ROMAN MARYPORT

There is a Roman fort at Maryport, just behind the Senhouse Roman Museum. The museum building is itself a historic building. It was built in 1855 and was formerly known as The Battery, being a naval gunnery training centre.

Most of the objects in the museum derive from the fort at Maryport and the Roman civil settlement attached to it. The museum displays the largest group of Roman military altar stones and inscriptions of any site in Britain and unique examples of Romano–British religious sculpture. The collection, which was begun by the Senhouse family in the 1570s, is the oldest in the country, and is of international importance.

Maryport is the birthplace of Thomas Henry Ismay, the founder of the Oceanic Steam Navigation Company, more commonly known as the White Star Line. His son was Joseph Bruce Ismay, who travelled on (and survived) the maiden voyage of his company's ocean liner, the RMS *Titanic* in 1912. Bruce Ismay suffered much criticism in later life because he survived, when many hundreds of woman and children drowned.

WORKINGTON

The port of Workington is the second port to be still working and being developed at the present time. Workington is still an industrial town, as its name might suggest. In the past mining, shipping and manufacturing were prominent. However, the town's original name comes from Weork and Wyre, an Anglian chieftain, and does not refer to its past industry. It was the development of the coal trade (from 1650 onwards) and the coming of the Industrial Revolution that changed Workington. High-quality haematite iron ore drew industry to the area and provided the impetus for the town's growth as an industrial centre.

It was at Workington that Henry Bessemer introduced his revolutionary steel-making process. During the eighteenth and nineteenth centuries more than thirty pits were in operation, and Workington remained the centre of steel production in north-west England for 100 years. A favourite local saying referred to the railway tracks made in Workington and exported to other countries as 'holding the world together'.

UPPIES AND DOWNIES GAME

Workington is well known for its very own legendary 'Uppies and Downies'. It is a version of Medieval football that takes place at Easter and can last several hours. The object is *to* 'hail the ball' (throw it up in the air three times) at the opposing team's goal. The Downies' goal is a capstan at the harbour, while the Uppies' is the gates of Workington Hall, Parklands. There are no other rules and the game is primarily a rough and tumble interspersed with breakaway sprints by members of one team or the other, with some similarities to rugby. Some players from outside Workington take part, especially fellow West Cumbrians, resulting in about 1,000 players on each team. An Uppies and Downies ball is made from four pieces of cow leather. It is 21in (53cm) in circumference and weighs about 2½lb (1.1kg). Only three handmade balls are produced every year and each is dated. The team names come from their geographical location in the town – 'Uppies' are the miners, and 'Downies' the sailors, though anyone else is welcome to take part, their team depending on where they hail from. The Cloffocks, the central open space recreation area, is recognised as the dividing line, and this is where the kick-off takes place.

2009 FLOODING IN WORKINGTON – A 1,000-YEAR EVENT!

The major flooding in Cumbria in 2005 was followed in 2009 by an even worse event in the west of Cumbria that led to the flooding of many properties. All four road and pedestrian bridges in Workington were either swept away, or severely damaged, leaving one sound railway bridge crossing the River Derwent in the town.

A particular tragedy that occurred at this time was the death of PC Bill Barker (previously mentioned on p19), who died saving the lives of motorists by directing them away from the crumbling Northside Bridge in Workington when it suddenly gave way beneath him at 4.40 a.m. on Friday, 20 November. His body was found on a beach in Allonby several hours later. A memorial to PC Barker was later unveiled at Curwen Park in the town.

WHITEHAVEN

The first mention of shipping in the area related to Whitehaven. It is recorded that in 1192 the Nevilles of Raby Castle in Durham joined Henry II on his expedition to Ireland and they asked Whitehaven to furnish shipping. A further record dated 1299 mentions that Alexander Scott, master of the *Marriot* of Whitehaven, and his five sailors were paid 14*s* for eight days' work carrying corn to mill at Whitehaven.

The payment was made up as follows: 3*d* per day sailors, 6*d* for masters.

Sailor's pay = 5 × 3 × 8 = 120*d*. Captain's pay = 6 × 8 = 48*d*. Total = 168*d* = 14*s* in old money. (240*d* = £1).

However, Whitehaven was dismissed in 1566 as consisting of six fisherman's cabins and a 10-ton vessel. Later the town was described as consisting of ten thatched cottages.

1642 etching of Whitehaven.

Then, in 1633, a letter from the king to the Lord Deputy, Dublin, described the port as very commodiously situated for Ireland and suitable for supplying it with coals, but that it was decayed and dangerous and had been the cause of the loss of many good ships. A pier would cost £600.

This was the beginning of Industrial Whitehaven with Sir Christopher Lowther, owner of the coal mines, who built the stone pier in 1634 for the burgeoning coal trade with Ireland. The first etching of Whitehaven dates back to 1642. It shows the 1634 pier with packhorses bringing coal to the harbour and the chapel.

By 1705 the town had grown to more than 2,000 inhabitants when a local captain sailed to Virginia and brought back a cargo of tobacco. A considerable tobacco trade soon built up with Virginia and Maryland. Tobacco auctions were held in Whitehaven. Emigrants were exported to the New World along with all materials needed to settle, and tobacco was brought back. By 1712, 1.6 million lb per year was imported, which increased to 4.4 million lb by 1740. The total for England and Wales was only 20 million lb. Hence, a quarter of all imported tobacco passed through Whitehaven.

THE SLAVE TRIANGLE

A less savoury side to this was that Whitehaven became involved in the slave trade due to the increased demand for rum and sugar from the Caribbean. Ships left Whitehaven with goods and trinkets to purchase slaves from the West African coast, who were then transported in terrible conditions to the Caribbean. The ships then returned home with rum and sugar, completing the triangle.

For ten years Whitehaven was very involved in this terrible trade until an abolition movement began around 1769. This swept through Whitehaven at an astounding pace, picking up supporters from every quarter, one of whom, surprisingly, was John Paul Jones. As a young man of 17 he was taken on as third mate on the ship *King George*, used in the slave trade. He hated it. Then two years later he was transferred to the *Two Friends* of Kingston, Jamaica, which was only 150ft long with a crew of six and carried seventy-seven negro slaves. It must have been a terrible journey. The smell from these 'Blackbirders', as they were called, could be detected for miles. He quit in disgust and was given free passage home on the *John of Kirkcudbright*, calling it an abominable trade.

John Paul is better known, of course, for his daring, but abortive, raid on Whitehaven during the American War of Independence (1775–83). In this night landing the USS *Ranger* stood 2 miles off the town and sent in two boats with thirty men, armed with pistols and cutlasses. They rowed against the tide for three hours, planning to destroy hundreds of ships by fire while they were stranded in port at low tide. They scaled the walls of the fort, burst into the guardhouse and secured it without bloodshed. Jones, with midshipman Joe Green, then went to spike the guns at the half moon battery – to protect their escape.

Lieutenant Wallingford and his men (who were to fire the ships) landed at Old Quay slip and headed straight for the pub to secure it and make sure no one left to raise the alarm. They then got drunk!

Jones returned to find that no ships had been fired as his own crew and Wallingford's had no lights, their candles having burnt out. Dawn was approaching so they gave up on the north harbour, secured a light from a house and made matches from canvas, sulphur and tar and threw them lit into the holds of several ships. Meanwhile one of his men, David Freeman, had started knocking on doors to warn residents their houses could be in danger! The town was prepared, however, with fire engines and managed to put out the fires in the few ships where the matches had taken hold.

By 1816, Whitehaven was ranked as the largest town in the north of England after Newcastle and York with a population of 10,000, of which 1,600 were sailors manning more than 200 ships.

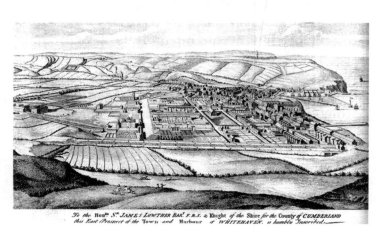

Matthias Reed's etching of Whitehaven.

Mathias Reed's 1738 etching of the town is the most famous view of early Whitehaven. Note the fine houses and the coal hurries, which were far beyond their time. These hurries and coal chutes had a capacity of 6,500 tons and people came from miles around to watch and hear the ships being loaded with 2 tons at a time (a wagon load) being tipped down the chutes. Whitehaven led the way in mechanisation. The Howgill Inclined Plane, built in 1813, was designed to replace forty men and horses. Loaded wagons, descending the hill to the hurries, pulled the empty ones up. The rotating wheels of the wagons pumped air into a cylinder, which applied the brakes. A bleed valve was adjusted to release air, thus controlling the speed of descent.

Shipbuilding was a major industry in Whitehaven in the eighteenth, nineteenth and early twentieth centuries. The largest ship launched was the *Alice E. Leigh* of 2,927 tons in 1889. Both she and the last ship at that time, the *Englehorn*, stuck on the slipway and had to be hauled into the water, causing the company to lose a great deal of money. It went bankrupt in 1890. At one time the demand for ships was so great that the industry expanded out into smaller ports such as Harrington. More than 1,000 ships were built, mostly colliers, the last in 1938.

Today, like Maryport, Whitehaven is an attractive tourist town with no major industry but a wealth of fine buildings and memories of its industrial and nautical past.

SEASCALE

Further down the coast the village of Seascale is encountered. The name is derived from *skali*, meaning in Norse a wooden hut or shelter. Many other Norse place names are to be found, including Seascale How, Skala Haugr (the hill near the shelter), and Whitriggs, *hvitihrgger* (the white ridge). As the Norsemen penetrated inland other *skalar* were named, so Seascale was distinguished by reference to the sea. However, little development occurred in Seascale until 1939, with the establishment of the Royal Ordnance factories at Sellafield and Drigg. At that time accommodation was built for munitions workers. Then, in 1947, after the Second World War, the huge nuclear building programme at the former Sellafield ordnance factory commenced. Seascale became a dormitory community for the Windscale and Calder Hall nuclear sites (later combined as Sellafield). As a result, in the 1950s it was known as 'the brainiest town in Britain'.

The noted Victorian author George Gissing based part of one of his novels, *The Odd Woman*, on Seascale and the Lake District. Gissing first visited in 1868/69 as a youngster, and although he only visited Seascale and the Lakes about four times, it left a tremendous impression on him, and he used material from his visits over the course of thirty years of writing.

FIRE AT WINDSCALE AND THE SUBSEQUENT COVER-UP

On the night of 10 October 1957, Britain was on the brink of an unprecedented nuclear tragedy. A fire ripped through the radioactive materials in the core of Windscale, Britain's first nuclear reactor. Tom Tuohy, the deputy general manager at the site, led the team faced with dealing with a nightmare no one had thought possible. 'Mankind had never faced a situation like this; there's no one to give you any advice,' he said. They were confronted by a terrifying dilemma. If they let the fire burn out, it could spread radioactivity over a large area of Britain. But if they put water on the reactor, they risked turning it into a nuclear bomb that could kill them all. 'I phoned the general manager,' Tuohy recalled, and said, 'Look, I want to turn on the water.'

'I thought, if it goes up, we will all go with it,' remembers Margaret Davis, whose husband Eddie was also engaged in the emergency operation. 'I've never been so frightened in my whole life.' Details of the inquiry into the disaster have only been released in the last few years. Scientists had been warning about the dangers of an accident for some time. The safety margins of the radioactive materials inside the reactor were being further and further eroded, but the politicians and the military ignored the warnings. Instead they increased demands on Windscale to produce material for an H-bomb.

At Windscale, Tuohy's gamble paid off. By turning on the water and shutting off the air, they managed to put out the fire and avert a tragedy. For fifty years, the official record on the accident has been that the very men who had averted a potentially devastating accident were to blame for causing it. 'I resented it at the time,' says Peter Jenkinson, who was an assistant physicist at the reactor, 'and I hoped the record would be put straight.' After the inquiry findings were released, he and his colleagues finally got their wish.

However, there was a legacy. A plume of radioactive isotopes, mainly iodine and caesium, swept over much the same area of the Lake District of Western Cumbria as that affected by the Chernobyl fallout thirty years later. This fire and its environmental effects were surrounded by a great deal of secrecy, although farmers in the vicinity were forced to pour away contaminated milk for several weeks. After the Chernobyl accident of April 1986, in Britain upland areas received heavy variable deposits of radioactive caesium isotopes. Within three months scientists and politicians alike decided that the initially wide restricted area in Cumbria (which included about 500 farms) should be reduced to a central crescent covering 150 farms. Very close to this central 'crescent' of longer-term radioactive contamination, almost suggesting itself as its focal point, is the Sellafield–Windscale nuclear complex. One local farmer said, 'They talk about these things coming from Russia, but it's surely no coincidence that it's gathered around Sellafield. They must think everyone is completely stupid.'

And another farmer ventured this explanation: 'Quite a lot of farmers around believe it's from Sellafield and not from Chernobyl at all. In 1957 it was a Ministry of Defence establishment – they kept things under wraps – and it was maybe much more serious than they gave out. Locals were drinking milk, which should probably never have been allowed – and memory lingers on.'

A little further down the coast is the village of Ravenglass. In the second century, it was an important naval base for the Romans. It is the most southerly point of the Cumbrian coastal defence system, an extension of Hadrian's Wall. Ravenglass was occupied by the Romans for more than 300 years and had a garrison of 500 soldiers. The village was a regional supply point for much of north-western Roman Britain, with a road from Ravenglass over the Hardknott Pass to the Roman forts at Hardknott and Ambleside. Today, there are few Roman remains, except for a bath house, known locally as Walls Castle. This is one of the largest remaining Roman structures in England. Ravenglass is the only coastal village in the Lake District National Park. It is also reputed to be a birthplace of Saint Patrick, competing with Banwen in South Wales!

Laal Ratty.

However, Ravenglass is best known as the terminus for Laal Ratty, the narrow-gauge Ravenglass and Eskdale Railway. The railway carries tens of thousands of visitors every year. The journey itself was one of Wainwright's favourites; crossing through 7 miles of spectacular scenery within sight of England's highest mountains, the Scafell Range.

Its origins lie with the nineteenth-century iron mines. In the early 1870s the Whitehaven Mining Company investigated the haematite deposits at Boot, near the head of the Eskdale valley. These were considered good enough to warrant the construction of a 3ft gauge railway to carry the ore from Eskdale to Ravenglass, from where it could be transferred to the Furness railway. The line was built and opened in 1875 and in 1876 it was decided to introduce a passenger service, opened by Lord Muncaster in November 1876. The line was soon christened Owd (or old) Ratty by the dalesfolk, who found it greatly improved their communication with the outside world. It soon became a popular tourist attraction. Unfortunately, the Whitehaven Mining Company failed in 1877 and the line was put into receivership. The receiver continued to operate Owd Ratty, mainly as a passenger service, for another thirty-four years until the remaining mines at Boot closed, which eventually led to the closure of the line after almost forty years.

Three years later, in 1915, it was proposed to reopen the line with a 15in gauge track and rolling stock by the Narrow Gauge Railway Company Ltd, and by 1917 trains were running and Owd Ratty was renamed Laal Ratty. The line is now owned and operated by the Ravenglass and Eskdale Steam Railway Company.

BARROW IN FURNESS AND WALNEY ISLAND

At the southern coastal tip of Cumbria lie Barrow in Furness and Walney Island. The name Barrow derives from the Norse *Barrai*, meaning either 'bare island' or 'island off the headland'.

THE OLDEST NORTHERNER

A new analysis of bones from a cave in this area of modern Cumbria has determined they are the earliest human bones known from Northern Britain. Kents Bank Cave, on the north side of Morecambe Bay, was excavated in the early 1990s and 2001. A fragment of human leg bone was found that has been radiocarbon dated to just over 10,000 years old, making it the earliest known human bone from northern Britain.

In July 2012 a fabulous Roman bracelet was found in the Dalton area of Furness. Nothing quite like this had been found there before. It is a silver bracelet dating from the second or third century AD, when the Romans controlled Britannia.

In the Middle Ages, Barrow in Furness was a small hamlet within the lands of Furness Abbey and by 1835 comprised just two wooden jetties, ten or a dozen cottages and two public houses. Then the iron prospector Henry Schneider arrived in 1839 and, with other investors, opened the Furness Railway to transport iron ore and slate from local mines to the coast. Factories for smelting and exporting steel followed and, by the late nineteenth century, the Barrow steelworks was the world's largest. By then the population had increased to 47,000. Barrow's rapid expansion from small fishing village to Victorian boom-town produced feelings of surprise and even awe from some onlookers. 'One of the miracles of our time; I look upon it with that same sort of wonder with which some people regard the pyramids.' (Bishop of Carlisle, 1871).

Natives of Barrow, and the local dialect, are known as Barrovian. It differs from the Cumbrian dialect as for many years Barrow was in Lancashire and has a lot in common with the Lancashire dialect.

BARROW AND SHIPBUILDING

Barrow has a long history of shipbuilding. The first ship launched by the shipyard was the passenger cargo ship the *Duke of Devonshire* in 1873. The yard soon gained a reputation for innovation that helped it win contracts for submarines, airships, liners, engines and armaments. The iron and steelmaking works closed after the Second World War, leaving Vickers shipyard as Barrow's main industry and employer.

Barrow shipyard remains operational as the UK's largest (by workforce) and is undergoing a major expansion associated with the Dreadnought submarine programme.

Situated on the northern edge of Morecambe Bay, Barrow is a hub for energy generation and handling. Offshore wind farms form one of the highest concentrations of turbines in the world. In 2011, Barrow's population was 57,000, the second largest urban area in Cumbria after Carlisle.

WALNEY ISLAND

Walney Island is part of Barrow in Furness and it is separated from mainland Barrow by Walney Channel, crossed by the Jubilee Bridge. It is the largest island of the Furness Islands group, both in population and size, as well as being the largest English island in the Irish Sea. Its population in 2011 was 10,651.

THE ISLANDS OF FURNESS

These little known islands are the third biggest group of islands in England. There are seven islands and two islets, four of which are populated. Piel Island has a castle as well as the King of Piel, who is the landlord of the island's public house, the Ship Inn. As well as the landlord and his family the island has three other permanent residents who live in the old Pilots Cottages. Barrow Island and the old Ramsey Islands are now part of the docks system.

Continuing this journey around Cumbria takes the reader north again to the central fells of the Helvellyn range. They lie to the south-east of Keswick overlooking the Vale of St John, Thirlmere Lake, Dunmail Raise, Grasmere and Rydal.

6

GRASMERE, AMBLESIDE AND THE CENTRAL FELLS

THIRLMERE AND MANCHESTER

To the north of Dunmail Raise is Thirlmere. In 1894 this lake had the dubious distinction of being the first in the district to be converted into a reservoir by the Manchester Corporation. Prior to the building of the dam, Thirlmere, formerly known as Leathes Water or Wythburn Water, consisted of two parts connected by a narrow and shallow channel. The hamlet of Armboth on the west side was connected by a bridge over this channel to Dale Head Park and the Keswick road.

Armboth, or City as it was known to the lead miners of Helvellyn, was to disappear forever with the raising of the water level. The later schemes at Haweswater and Ullswater were required to blend in with the natural environment and not to alter the natural beauty of the area. The Thirlmere scheme, however, was not bound by such tight constraints. As a result, for many years access was denied to the lake and visitors were discouraged. Unsightly notices prohibiting trespass on water board land were commonly encountered. Happily this is no longer the situation. The signs have disappeared and

North West Water has constructed paths and stiles giving easy access to the lake and the surrounding woods. Whatever one thinks of the spoiling of the area by these nineteenth-century engineers, one can only admire their vision and engineering skills. The aqueduct that carries Thirlmere's water the 96 miles to Manchester is a series of tunnels, buried channels and pipelines that utilise gravity alone to keep the water moving.

KING DUNMAIL AND DUNMAIL RAISE

That pile of stones heaped over brave Dunmail's bones
He who had my supreme command
Last king of rocky Cumberland

(Wordsworth's 'Waggoner')

In popular legend the cairn at the summit of Dunmail Raise marks the burial place of King Dunmail. The story of King Dunmail and his last battle at Dunmail Raise in AD 945 is steeped in Arthurean legend. There are several versions of the story, some more fanciful than others. The description here is a compilation of these.

Dunmail was the son of Owain, one of the strongest of the Cumbrian kings who came to the throne about AD 920. Owain was descended from the old Caesarian line of the kings of Strathclyde, who by this time had lost much of their power and influence due to attacks from Anglian invaders, who encroached into the Scottish lowlands. Owain ruled his kingdom from Penrith as Carlisle had been sacked by the Danes in AD 876 and was a ruin. The seven tombs forming the Giant's Grave and the Giant's Thumb in Penrith churchyard date back to this time and indicate that the town of Penrith was an important centre. The popular tradition that says the monuments are the tomb of a giant, Hugh or Owen Caesarius, probably records some dim memory of Owain. Minstrels through the ages might have sung of Owain as a 'great man', even 'a giant of a man'. It would be quite easy for such a ballad to become associated with the obelisks in the churchyard, which might have been then seen as the grave of this 'giant'.

Owain, together with his uncle, King Constantine II of the Scots, plotted with the Vikings of Galloway and the Isles against the English King Athelstan, to whom they had previously sworn allegiance as King of all Britain. This led to a great battle on the flat-topped mountain near Ecclefechan in Galloway, called Burnswark, at which the English were victorious. What happened to Owain after the battle is not recorded, but Dunmail, his son and successor, apparently did not learn from this experience. Dunmail continued his dangerous alliance with the Vikings of Galloway and the Isles. King Edmund, the Saxon king, who succeeded Athelstan on the English throne, was quick to act, sending an army across Stainmore that defeated Dunmail at a place unknown. After this battle, Edmund, with the usual barbarity of the times, put out the eyes of Dunmail's two sons and gave his country to Malcolm, King of Scotland, on condition he preserved peace in the northern parts of England. Although several sites for the battle have been suggested, including Orrest Head at Windermere, legend and popular belief portray Dunmail Raise as the battleground. The story of the battle is interwoven with legend and superstition but is a fine tale to hear. I quote from an account given in 1927 in *Cycling* magazine by one W.T. Palmer:

> The Raise has legend of one mighty battle a thousand years ago. King Edmund the Saxon was quelling the raider Britons on his border, and Dunmail of Cumberland came in for punitive attention. The armies met on this level among the hills, and a formless pile of stones marks the burial place of those who fell. Here is a pretty legend: The crown of Dunmail of Cumberland was charmed, giving its wearer a succession in his kingdom. Therefore King Edmund the Saxon coveted it above all things. When Dunmail came to the throne of the mountain land a wizard in Gilsland Forest held a master charm to defeat the promise of his crown. He Dunmail slew. The magician was able to make himself invisible save at cock crow and to destroy him the hero braved a cordon of wild wolves at night. At the first peep of dawn, he entered the cave where the wizard was lying. Leaping to his feet the magician called out, 'Where river runs north or south with the storm,' ere Dunmail's sword silenced him.
>
> The story came to the ear of the covetous Saxon, who, after much enquiry of his priests, found that an incomplete curse, although powerful against Dunmail, could scarcely hurt another holder of the crown. Spies were accordingly sent into Cumbria to find where a battle could be fought favourable to the magician's words. On Dunmail Raise, in times of storm even in unromantic today, the torrent sets north or south in

capricious fashion. The spies found the place, found also fell land chiefs who were persuaded to become secret allies of the Saxon. The campaign began. Dunmail moved his army south to meet the invader, and they joined battle in the pass. For long hours the battle was with the Cumbrians; the Saxons were driven down the hill again and again. As his foremost tribes became exhausted, Dunmail retired and called on his reserves – they were mainly the ones favouring the southern king. On they came, spreading in well – armed lines from side to side of the hollow way, but instead of opening to let the weary warriors through, they delivered an attack on them. Surprised, the army reeled back and their rear was attacked with redoubled violence by the Saxons. The loyal ranks were forced to stand back to back round their king; assailed by superior forces they fell rapidly, and ere long the brave chief was shot down by a traitor of his own bodyguard:

'My crown,' cried he, 'bear it away; never let the Saxon flaunt it.'

A few stalwarts took the charmed treasure from his hands, and with a furious onslaught made the attackers give way. Step by step they fought their way up the ghyll of Dunmail's beck – broke through all resistance on the open fell, and, aided by a dense cloud, evaded their pursuers. Two hours later the faithful few met by Grisedale Tarn, and consigned the crown to its depths – 'till Dunmail come again to lead us'. And every year the warriors come back, draw up the magic circlet from the depths of the wild mountain tarn, and carry it with them over Seat Sandal to where the king is sleeping his age long sleep. They knock with his spear on the topmost stone of the cairn and from its heart comes a voice, 'Not yet; not yet – wait a while my warriors.'

The cairn can still be seen in the central reservation on the summit of Dunmail Raise.

A modern postscript to this story occurred in the 1960s, when the county council was improving the road from Keswick to Ambleside. At the top of Dunmail Raise the contractors began removing the cairn. They were quickly stopped by the uproar caused when local historians realised what was happening to this symbol of their heritage. A compromise was quickly reached and a 300m stretch of dual carriageway was constructed with the cairn in the central reservation.

HELVELLYN

Although not the highest, Helvellyn (the Hill of Willan) is probably the best known mountain in Lakeland. This is more likely due to the attraction of the Striding and Swirral Edges than to its own grandeur. Helvellyn is the high point of a meandering ridge that rises in the north at Clough Head, and traverses the Dodds and Raise to the rounded and rather featureless summit dome of Lakeland's second highest mountain. From here the ridge continues south over Nethermost and Dollywaggon Pikes, dropping briefly to Grisedale Tarn, before rising to the stony summit of Fairfield. A gentle descent over Rydal Fell then follows until valley level is reached once more at Rydal Water.

There are many steep crags and rocky precipices to the east of the summit ridge and care must be taken in poor visibility or winter conditions. Many people over the years have taken the quick route to Red Tarn from the summit plateau, often with disastrous results:

A serious young lady from Welwyn
took a cookery book up Helvellyn.
While reading the recipes
She fell down a precipice,
And that was the end of poor Ellen!

(*Lakeland Limericks*, Gibbs 1942)

Red Tarn from the approach to Striding Edge.

Another explanation of the name Helvellyn is 'the hill that forms the wall or defence of the lake'. This derives from the Norse *Hel* (Hill), *Gival* (Well) and *Lyn* (Lake). Literally this could be 'the hill containing the lake which is like a well'.

This line of mountains can be thought of as the backbone of the Lake District running north to south and separating east from west. The valleys ringing the Helvellyn range are rich in local history. There are stories of myth and legend in the early border battles. There are tales of the lives of the lake poets, who did so much to popularise and romanticise the Lake District in the early nineteenth century. Finally, there is the influence of industry on the people and the landscape. The remains of lead and iron mines still scar the fells, silent reminders of once-thriving industries that, before the age of tourism, were the lifeblood of the district. Later the water industry left its mark, with the creation of the Thirlmere reservoir during the last quarter of the nineteenth century.

MEMORIALS OF HELVELLYN

There are three memorials on Helvellyn:
(i) The first of these is encountered as one crosses Striding Edge. A white-painted iron plaque marks the spot where Robert Dixon of Rookings, Patterdale, died on 27 May 1858, while following the Patterdale Foxhounds.
ii) The second memorial on Helvellyn is to be found 100 yards or so south of the summit shelter beside the path leading towards Wythburn. A plaque records the

first landing of an aircraft on the summit of an English mountain. On 22 December 1926, pilots John Leeming and Bert Hinkler landed an Avro 585 Gosport aeroplane on the summit plateau. After a short stay they then flew back to Woodford in Cheshire (Woodford is very near the present Manchester Airport).

(iii) The third memorial, which stands on the summit plateau of Helvellyn directly above Red Tarn, records an event that has since become famous through the attentions of the Lakeland poets. A large memorial stone, set into a cairn, records the death of John Gough of Manchester, who perished in the spring of 1805 when attempting to cross from Patterdale to

John Gough's memorial stone on the summit of Helvellyn. Erected by Canon Rawnsley in 1899.

Wythburn. A fall of snow had partially obscured the path and he apparently fell from the head of Red Cove on to the rocks below. His dog, which accompanied him on that fateful day, remained with the body until it was found three months later by William Harrison of Hartsop. It was this act of extreme devotion that captured the imagination of both Wordsworth and Scott. Scott's verses on 'Helvellyn' refer to the event and Wordsworth's famous poem 'Fidelity' tells the tale in full.

Here is an abbreviated version:

A barking sound the shepherd hears, A cry as of a dog or fox; He halts and searches with his eyes, Among the scattered rocks: And now at distance can discern – A stirring in a brake or fern; And instantly a dog is seen, Glancing through that covert green … The shepherd stood; then makes his way – Towards the dog, o'er rocks and stones, As quickly as he may; Not far had gone before he found – A human skeleton on the ground; The appalled discoverer with a sigh – Looks round to learn the history … From those abrupt and perilous rocks – The man had fallen, that place of fear! At length upon the shepherds mind It breaks, and all is clear: He instantly recalled the name, And who he was, and whence he came; Remembered, too, the very day – On which the traveller passed this way … The dog which still was hovering nigh, Repeating the same timid cry, This dog had been through three month's space – A dweller in that savage place. Yes, proof was plain that since the day, When this ill-fated traveller died, The dog had watched about the spot, Or by his master's

side – How nourished here through such long time –
He knows who gave that love sublime: And gave that
strength of feeling great – Above all human estimate.

John Gough, a Quaker, was buried in the village of
Tirril, between Penrith and Ullswater.

A later writer on this event caused some controversy.
Professor Wilson of Edinburgh University (who wrote
under the pseudonym of Christopher North as the
editor of *Blackwoods* magazine) was a great friend of
Auld Will Ritson of Wasdale. We will hear of both of
them later in this book.

Wilson's light-hearted tale of that event talked about
the Red Tarn club of ravens, who were fabled to have set
to work on the Quaker's body. This upset many people,
who preferred the tale of the fox terrier protecting
its master from predators. There is speculation how
Foxey survived for three months on the mountain.
Canon Rawnsley in his book *Literary Associations of
the English Lakes*, disputes the suggestion that Foxey
ate the remains of her master. He quotes a letter dated
'Yanwath 30th of Eighth month 1805' that contains a
brief note of the incident. In that letter, written only six
months after the event, it is stated that 'his bones were
bleached white though covered with his clothes, and his
skull was separated and found at a distance from the
rest … His faithful dog had attended his relics between
three and four months, but how it had subsisted itself
is difficult to suppose, though it appeared to the people
who collected his remains that "it ate grass".' Foxey
gave birth to pups during her vigil, which were found
dead. Further evidence, says Rawnsley, that Foxey

survived only on grass and carrion mutton, which did not provide enough sustenance to support her pups.

GRASMERE AND WORDSWORTH

Grasmere is probably best known as the home of the Romantic poet William Wordsworth, who did so much through his writings to popularise and protect the Lake District that we know today. He travelled a lot in his earlier years but lived at Dove Cottage, Grasmere, with his sister Dorothy Wordsworth from 1799–1808. Incidentally, Dove Cottage was the home of author Thomas De Quincey, from 1809–20. See the section on Wetheral in this book.

Rydal Mount, near Ambleside, was William Wordsworth's best-loved family home for the greater part of his life from 1813 to his death in 1850 at the age of 80. However, many of Wordsworth's best-known poems touch on his life at Grasmere. William had a brother John, a sea captain, who visited him at Dove Cottage when he returned from sea. When returning to his ship William would see his brother on his way, accompanying him as far as Grisedale Tarn, on the path over to Patterdale.

The inscribed stone that stands just off the path, a short distance east of Grisedale Tarn, marks the spot where William bade goodbye to his brother John for the last time. Unfortunately, shortly after this last parting, John was to perish in the loss of his ship, the East Indiaman, the *Earl of Abergavenny*. On Friday night, 5 February 1805, the ship was wrecked on The Shambles, off Portland Bill, through the incompetency of the pilot.

Wordsworth records this sad happening in a poem of lament, composed at the parting stone. There follows a short excerpt, verses 1 and 3:

The sheep boy whistled loud and lo! That instant, startled by the shock, the buzzard mounted from the rock Deliberate and slow: Lord of the air, he took his flight: Oh! Could he on that woeful night Have lent his wing, my brother dear, For one poor moment's space to thee And all that struggled with the sea When safety was so near.

Here we did stop and here look round, While each into his self descends, For that last thought of parting friends That is not to be found ...

The Parting Stone.

D. LUSH

Another Wordsworth poem relating to a family the poet probably knew was 'Michael'. This pathetic tale is too long to reproduce in full here. I will relate a brief synopsis of it:

Long ago a shepherd called Michael was married to a wife, Isabel, twenty years his junior. They were blessed late in life with an only son called Luke. From the age of 10 Luke worked with his father, who was then 66, day in and day out. In the evening they would rest in their cottage, which was high on the side of Greenhead Ghyll and could be seen from Grasmere and the surrounding vale. Every night Isabel lit a lamp to see them home, which, as it stood in the window of the cottage, could be seen by the whole valley. This light became famous and was named 'the Evening Star' by the residents of Grasmere Vale.

Unfortunately, due to the misfortune of his brother's son who failed in business, Michael, who had agreed to be bound in surety for his nephew, had to give up half of his living to cover the debt. The farm could no longer support both him and his son. Luke had to leave and live with a relative in the city, who agreed to try and find work for the lad. Before Luke left, his father and he laid the foundations of a new sheepfold beside the ghyll that, Michael promised, would be ready for his son's return, when his fortune was made. While his son was away Michael added to the sheepfold in his spare moments, ever looking forward to Luke's eventual return. Alas it was not to be. Luke soon became influenced by city life and turned to drink, gambling and coarse living. The old man lost heart when he heard the news and realised that Luke was not coming back. Michael finally died at the age of 91, with the sheepfold still unfinished. Isobel survived a further few years before the estate was sold and went into a stranger's hands. Wordsworth relates how the cottage, which was named the 'Evening Star', has gone, yet the oak is left that grew beside the door.

In recent years the author found a possible site for the cottage immediately west of Alcock Tarn where the remains of a house built into the hillside is to be seen. A few yards further down the slope, to the right of the cottage, are the rotten remains of a large tree stump. The view from this point is just as the poem describes, encompassing Grasmere Vale, Easedale and Dunmail Raise. About 500m north from this point at the junction with Rowantree Beck there is an incomplete sheepfold. Directly opposite, on the wooded hillside above the Swan Inn, the field is called Michael's Fold (on the current OS maps). All of this supports the proposition that the poem 'Michael' was about a family Wordsworth knew, living above Grasmere at that time.

BROWNRIGG WELL

One need never be thirsty on the summit of Helvellyn, even in the hottest weather. About 300ft below and 300 yards due west of the trig point is a never-failing spring called Brownrigg Well. The well is the source of a small stream that runs down into Whelpside Gill. However, in the nineteenth century the water was diverted by wooden water leat northwards and down into Mines Gill to serve Helvellyn lead mine. All traces of the dam have gone but the route of the leat is still visible as a narrow groove in the hillside. Mr H. Wilkinson of

Penrith, writing in *Cumbria* magazine in 1954 aged 90, described how, in his younger days around 1900–10, he always stopped at the well to partake of its icy cold water. At that time there was an iron cup, fixed by a chain, provided for the thirsty walker. Regrettably, as might be expected, the cup is no longer there.

An interesting but very steep route down from Helvellyn is to follow the line of the water leat into Mines Gill and descend through the remains of Wythburn lead mine. The upper and lower levels are encountered first with their spoil heaps. Below the lower level are the remains of the drum house and self-activating incline that took the ore in trucks to the ore dressing mill above the road. Across the beck are the remains of the smithy and the mine office. In the large stones at the entrance to the smithy one can see drill holes made when the smith was testing the drills he had just sharpened. Further down, where a small stream joins the main gill from the south, there are the remains of an early flush toilet! Over the stream one can see the remains of a small stone building such that the stream flows in at one side and out at the other. A wooden earth closet seat, strategically placed, was all that was needed for a flushing toilet without the need to pull the chain. They were obviously copying the Romans. Even further down was the powder house in the woods above the ore dressing mill. Alen McFadzean, a mine exploration friend of mine in the 1980s, has written a book about this mine. He told me that during the war a German spy must have hidden himself here with his Morse transmitter, which was found in a small suitcase in the building after the war.

SKIING IN CUMBRIA

To the north of Helvellyn is the hill called Raise, the home of the Lakeland Ski Club. Founded in 1936, the Lake District Ski Club operates a 360m button tow giving access to a substantial part of the mountain. There are up to nine distinct pistes available, depending on prevailing conditions, the longest of which is almost a mile. The downside is that to reach the tow one must walk up about a mile from the Glenridding valley. North of Raise, on the other side of Sticks Pass are the Dodds and Clough Head. These rounded hills are fine for cross-country skiing when conditions are right. The only other ski club in Cumbria is the Carlisle club, who have a dry slope in Carlisle and a slope at Yad Moss near Alston in the Pennines. Yad Moss has the longest lift in England, and a day lodge. The long wide slopes and varied terrain are ideal for snowboarders and skiers alike. However, the long lift and fairly steep slopes make this mountain less suitable for beginners.

When looking over Grasmere from Dove Cottage, Helm Crag stands out to the north with its distinctive rocky ridge silhouetted against the sky. Over the years people have named these rocks according to their fancy. The most common name is the Lion and the Lamb but others such as the 'old lady playing an organ' and the 'howitzer' are also in use. One might suppose it depends to a certain extent on your viewpoint, as the ridge is visible from the top of Dunmail Raise all the way down to the south of Grasmere. A poem (or limerick), certainly not written by Wordsworth when he lived at Rydal Mount, follows:

A professor of physics at Rydal
Would maintain the lakes were all tidal,
And to this he adhered,
Though the scientists jeered
And assured him his theories were idle.

(*Lakeland Limericks*, Gibbs, 1942)

GRASMERE SPORTS

Most of the villages among the Lakeland Hills have their annual meets and sports days but none are as well-known as the Grasmere Sports, held in August when the weather can be changeable to say the least. Here the traditional local sports are kept alive such as Cumberland wrestling, hound trailing and the guides' race. The sports day began as a separate event from the autumn fair in 1859 but Cumberland wrestling began long before that. The most popular event at Grasmere Sports is the guides' race, to the top of Silver Howe and back. First held in 1868 it was won by G. Birkett. Other events at that meeting were wrestling, high jumping, pole vaulting, flat races and a boat race. So it was a true 'sports' meeting.

AMBLESIDE

A few miles south of Grasmere is the Lakeland town of Ambleside. Like Keswick it is now essentially a tourist town. The name is from the old Norse *Á-mel-sætr*, which literally translates as 'river – sandbank

– summer pasture'. Ambleside sits at the northern end of Windermere and when the railway came to Windermere village (much to the chagrin of Wordsworth and others) tourism in the town developed quickly, with steamer services linking Ambleside to Bowness and Lakeside.

The Roman fort of Galava, dating from AD 79 is on the northern shore of Windermere at Waterhead, Ambleside. During the Industrial Revolution Ambleside became a centre for producing charcoal, used in smelting the iron ore of Furness and west Cumbria, and timber for the production of bobbins for the textile industry. Water power was in use at an early stage and later machine tools were manufactured here. The old packhorse trail between Ambleside and Grasmere, around Loughrigg Terrace, was originally the main route between Ambleside and Grasmere (the modern road only dates from 1770). It was also used to carry the deceased (another corpse road) from Rydal and Ambleside for burial in Grasmere Church (before St Mary's Church in Ambleside was consecrated in 1854). Smithy Brow at the end of the trail was where pack ponies were reshod after their journey.

There are other interesting facts about Loughrigg. The nomadic journalist, Thomas De Quincey (1785–1859), who was mentioned earlier as living at Dove Cottage, Grasmere, lived at Fox Ghyll, Loughrigg from 1820–25. Here he wrote *Confessions of an English Opium Eater* (1822) and contributed to the *London Magazine*.

Matthew Arnold met Charlotte Bronte and Harriet Martineau at Loughrigg Holme, the home of poet Edward Quillinan and Dora (Wordsworth's daughter) in 1850.

William Wordsworth worked in Ambleside at The Old Stamp House from 1813–43 when he was Distributor of Stamps for Westmorland. In 1842 he became Poet Laureate and resigned this office.

In 1818, John Keats visited and stayed at The Salutation Hotel in Lake Street and, in 1835, both Alfred, Lord Tennyson, when he was working on 'Morte d'Arthur', and Edward Fitzgerald stayed at the hotel, which is still open today.

Harriet Martineau (1802–76) has been quoted elsewhere in this book, a journalist, pamphleteer and novelist, she was a friend of Darwin. She built The Knoll, Ambleside, where she lived and wrote from April 1846 until her death. Wordsworth helped with the garden landscaping, planting two pine trees and chose the inscription for her sundial. Charlotte Bronte stayed for a week in 1850. Harriet Martineau campaigned locally for improved housing, sanitation and drainage. This led, in 1849, to the formation of the first building society in the north of England.

ELTERWATER

Travelling westwards from Ambleside takes one towards Elterwater and the Langdale valleys. Elterwater became famous for its gunpowder factory. Ian Tyler in his book *The Gunpowder Mills of Cumbria* tells how David Huddleston, who founded the Elterwater gunpowder works, took over the reins from a son who had died young. He soon found that the industry was a perilous one, for in a letter dated August 1827, he stated that he had had three serious 'blow ups' in the space of two months. However, business flourished, with mining companies on Alston Moor among the customers, and the Elterwater works were expanded. A dam had to be constructed to provide an adequate water supply, and Tyler records that its completion was marked by a wheelbarrow race down the fellside for the navvies, the first home getting two gallons of ale as his prize.

The most famous resident of Elterwater was Lanty Slee, quarryman and whisky distiller. Lancelot lived there more than 100 years ago and worked at the Elterwater slate quarry. He was a colourful character who became famous for his clandestine whisky distilling and his ability to avoid the excise men. Much of the whisky distilling took place in a small cave high up on Lingmoor above Little Langdale. Lanty's exploits have probably become embroidered and enlarged on with time but there is no doubt that he was quite successful in his illegal pursuits.

His cave high up on the hillside was close to a stream, which provided his water supply. Here he could distil his spirit in relative safety, relying on the wind and mist to disguise the occasional emissions of steam. Apparently this was only one of several locations where Lanty distilled his whisky. He is reputed to have had a still under the floor of his kitchen at Low Arnside Farm. The telltale steam from this device was led underground through a long pipe to emerge in a hedge in the adjoining field.

Having produced his whisky he had to market it. This was achieved by smuggling the spirit out at the dead of night by packhorse, across Slater's Bridge and up the fellside to another cave high on the slopes of

Wetherlam. From here he could watch the road over Wrynose Pass and choose his time to make his run for Ravenglass and the sea. Smuggling was a favourite pastime for many at this time. Duty free contraband run ashore along the coast could be bartered for illicit whisky and locally poached salmon. Lanty was not always successful in escaping detection and, every now and then, he would end up before the magistrates at Hawkshead. However, this did not appear to deter him, possibly because these same magistrates were some of his best customers. Lanty ranged far and wide in the district, having stills and whisky caches in many remote places. Perhaps one of these was in the area of Lanty's Tarn near Glenridding, Ullswater. The author knows of no other reason for the name.

GREAT LANGDALE, DUNGEON GHYLL AND THE OLD WOMAN'S GRAVE

Travelling on westwards from Elterwater via Chapel Stile one enters Great Langdale with its two well-known hotels. The Old Dungeon Ghyll Hotel and the New Hotel. The Old Dungeon Ghyll Hotel was originally a farm and an inn. In the rate book of 1885, it was named as Middlefell Inn and run by John Bennett, who was a well-known guide for tourists. These were the days of the horse-drawn 'charas' bringing visitors from Little Langdale over Blea Tarn Pass. They would stop at the top and blow their horn, a signal to get lunch or tea ready – the number of blasts informed the staff of the number of passengers requiring the meal!

The Old Woman's Grave.

The head of Great Langdale is enclosed on all sides by high mountains, the Langdale Pikes to the north, Bowfell and Crinkle Crags to the west and Pike O' Blisco to the south. The ridge of Crinkle Crags, surprisingly, derives its name from the Norse *kringla* or circle and not from its jagged appearance. A popular route to Scafell from Langdale follows Rosset Ghyll up to Angle Tarn. Beside the path about halfway up the ghyll is the Old Woman's Grave. The grave is now marked by a stone cross, pointing south-east, on a raised flat area to the left of the path. Originally it was a row of flat stones, according to an account of 1851:

> high up above the vale of Great Langdale we came to the Old Woman's Grave. Tradition relates that a Westmoreland woman, who was in the practice, for many years, of going over into Cumberland to receive an annuity, perished in the mountains. She was buried on the spot, and a row of flat stones marks her grave. My guide pointed to the hollow, a few yards below, where the body is said to have been found.

Alfred Wainwright mentioned the grave in his book on the Southern Fells. His story is at variance with Hudson's account of 1851. Wainwright said that according to Mr H. Mounsey of Skelwith, the old woman was a 'pack woman', who called at Langdale farms about 170 years ago selling her wares until, one fateful day, she perished on the hills. Hudson's account was written about fifty years after the event and his informant was his guide, the son of a Langdale farmer. This is another story that has been altered in the telling. Readers must decide for themselves which is most likely to be the accurate version.

STONE AXE FACTORY

In the Neolithic period Langdale had a productive stone axe industry sited on the upper scree slopes of Pike O' Stickle. The area has outcrops of fine-grained greenstone suitable for making polished axes, which have been found distributed across the British Isles.

LITTLE LANGDALE AND WRYNOSE AND HARDKNOTT PASSES

In the past Little Langdale was at the intersection of packhorse routes leading north, south, east and west to all the major towns in the area. Slater's Bridge which crosses the River Brathay, supported by a large mid-stream boulder and stone causeways, is a sixteenth century, slate-built, former packhorse bridge on one of these routes. The valley has been heavily mined and quarried over several hundred years, particularly for copper and the local green slate. Lanty Slee, the notorious whisky distiller and smuggler, mentioned earlier, made his home here. In 1840, Slee built Greenbank Farm in the valley.

The main road to the west is the Roman road, which climbs over Wrynose Pass and Hardknott Pass, (passing Hardknott Roman fort) to descend into Eskdale and on to Ravenglass. This is one of England's most challenging roads with very steep gradients and hairpin bends. There have been many accidents there in the past. One I remember made national television at the time. A truck and trailer, with the Spar logo on it, got stuck on one of the hairpin bends, blocking the road completely. It took two recovery firms, working together, to rescue it.

7

WINDERMERE, BOWNESS AND THE SOUTH-WESTERN FELLS

DUNNERDALE AND SEATHWAITE TARN

After climbing Wrynose Pass one can avoid Hardknott Pass by turning left at Cockley Beck and following the River Duddon down Dunnerdale to Broughton in Furness. A couple of miles down this road is a car park from where one can walk in Dunnerdale Forest on the right or follow the track to Seathwaite Tarn on the left.

Vicars and curates had a hard time in the eighteenth century. Livings carried very small stipends and the poor cleric depended greatly on the local population and his own wits to survive. One or two were so successful in this endeavour that they became part of the local folklore. One such example was the Reverend Richard Birkett, vicar of Martindale, who took unfair advantage of his parishioners. His story is told later in this book. An even more famous cleric was Robert Walker of Seathwaite, who was most benevolent to his parishioners, and became known as 'Wonderful Walker'.

Robert Walker is first recorded as taking up the posts of curate and schoolmaster at Buttermere in 1772. His salary was paid almost entirely in kind, as follows:

A 'Darrack' of peats, i.e. 'a day's work of peats'. This meant as much turf as he could dig upon the common moss in a day.

A 'Goose Grass'. This was the right of putting upon the fell or common ground a goose, a gander and their goslings for free pasture.

A 'Harden Sark'. This was the obligation of each of his parishioners to provide the curate with a part of his clothing. A Harden Sark was a shirt of very rough and coarse linen.

Mr Walker was engaged to instruct the children and perform the clerical duty of the parish, on condition that the parishioners would provide him with board and lodging. It was agreed that he should live at each of their houses for a week or a fortnight in the year. This agreement was known as 'The Right of Whittle Gate'. Many would have found this mode of living very uncomfortable but not Wonderful Walker, who used it to get to know his flock, to assess their assets and failings and to remove their prejudices. These emoluments of office, however only provided the bare essentials of life. Walker was the equivalent of the modern workaholic and his devotion to his calling was praised and recorded by several people of note, including Wordsworth.

The following passages from *Seathwaite and the Wonderful Walker* by Thomas Ellwood give an idea of his lifestyle:

In the mornings before school time, and in the evenings he laboured in manual occupations; during the day he taught school. He publicly catechised the children, and performed the whole duty, morning and afternoon on a Sunday. In summer he rose between three and four o'clock and went to the field with his scythe and his rake; and in harvest time with his sickle. He ploughed; he planted; he went on the mountains after the sheep; he sheered and salved them; he dug peat [...] all for hire [...] He was an excellent spinner of linen and cotton thread. All his own clothes and afterwards those of his family were of his own spinning. He knit and mended his own stockings, and made his own shoes. In his walks he never neglected to gather the wood from the hedges and bring it home.

He was also the physician and lawyer of the place; he drew up all wills, conveyances, bonds, &c., wrote all letters and settled all accounts. These labours (at all times considerable), at one period of the year, viz., between Christmas and Candlemas, when many transactions are settled in this country, were so intense that he passed a great part of the night and sometimes whole nights at his desk.

In December 1734, Robert took up the curacy of Torver. He stayed there just over a year before taking up the living at his native Seathwaite. Torver was a much better living with a salary of between 5 and 6 pounds a year, but Walker preferred to live in his home vale. Here he settled, married and built up the reputation previously described. He died in June 1802, aged 93, two years after the death of his wife.

Following the A591 road south from Ambleside, alongside the lake, takes one to Windermere and Bowness-on-Windermere.

WINDERMERE AND BOWNESS

Bowness-on-Windermere is the most 'touristy' town in the Lake District. One might think of it as the 'Blackpool of the Lake District', ideal for day trippers but to be avoided at all costs by those that love the Lake District for its beauty, unspoilt hills and valleys. Windermere village, which lies to the east of Bowness, did not exist until the arrival of the Kendal and Windermere's branch line in 1847. The station was built in an area of open fell and farmland. The nearest farm was Birthwaite, which gave its name to the station and the village that began to grow up near it. In about 1859, the residents began to call their new village by the name of Windermere, much to the chagrin of the people of Bowness, which had been the centre of the parish of Windermere for many centuries.

Windermere is the largest natural lake in England and has eighteen islands, the largest of which is Belle Island. Steamer passenger services operate along the whole length of the lake. These services date back to the former Furness Railway, who built the Lakeside branch.

WINDERMERE CHAIN FERRY AND THE 'CRIER OF THE CLAIFE'

There has been a ferry at the site of the current Windermere Ferry (halfway down the lake) for more than 500 years. The earliest craft were rowed across the lake, whilst later ferries were steam powered and, more recently, diesel powered. The ferry is a chain ferry such that two fixed chains are laid cross the lake and the ferry drives on these chains (Nowadays cables are more often used). Today the ferry is owned and operated by Cumbria County Council and is part of the B5285 road from Hawkshead on the west side to Crook on the east side.

On the west side of the ferry the high ground to the north is called Claife Heights, where the troubled ghost of a Cistercian monk from Furness Abbey wanders. His quest was to save the souls of immoral women but the temptations of the flesh overthrew the aspirations of the spirit and he fell madly in love with one of his charges, abandoning his vows and pursuing her to the heights of Claife. She shunned his advances and the rejection destroyed him. He spent the rest of his days wandering the Heights wailing in anguish. When his weakening body gave up the ghost, it proved to be one the grave could not contain, and his tortured soul continued to haunt the woods with wailing cries. Fearing no good could come from a meeting with the spectral Crier of Claife, the ferrymen of Bowness chose to ignore his blood-chilling summons whenever they came echoing across the lake after dark. But eventually, a young recruit arrived who laughed at their superstition. Whether out of bravado or a noble concern that the plaintive cries might belong to the living, the fearless newcomer heeded the call and set out across the choppy waters.

When he returned, his boat held no passenger – at least none the mortal eye could see. But he was fatally deranged: his eyes wide in terror and his powers of speech utterly lost – all he could manage was to shake and sob in abject fear. He died two days later without ever regaining the power to describe what he saw. Naturally this raised considerable alarm among the locals and another monk was summoned from Lady Holme Island to perform an exorcism. As darkness fell and the howls once more sent shivers down the spines of the ferrymen, the monk rowed out with a Bible and a bell. The demented spirit proved a powerful adversary and, despite his best efforts, the monk was unable to exorcise the ghoul completely, but he did succeed in confining it to an old quarry where he compelled it to stay until such a day 'as men walk dry shod across Windermere'. So maybe you should not worry too much unless you inadvertently visit that quarry after dark.

HILL TOP FARM AND BEATRIX POTTER

On the west side of the ferry are the villages of Near Sawrey and Far Sawrey. Beatrix Potter, best known for her children's books such as *The Tale of Peter Rabbit*, was already quite famous in 1905 when she bought Hill Top Farm in Near Sawrey. What is not so well known about Beatrix is her study of, and the watercolours she painted of, fungi, which led to her being widely respected in the field of mycology. Many of her best-known books were written at Hill Top Farm which, as a result, attracts thousands of visitors every year.

Her ambition to own land in the Lake District and to preserve it from development was encouraged by William Heelis, a local solicitor, who she married in 1913, at the age of 47. They became deeply involved in the community, Beatrix served on committees to improve rural living, opposed hydroplanes on Lake Windermere, founded a nursing trust to improve local health care, and developed a passion for breeding and raising Herdwick sheep.

In 1923 she bought Troutbeck Park, an enormous but disease-ridden sheep farm, which she restored to agricultural health. She became one of the most admired Herdwick breeders in the region and won prizes at all the local shows. The Heelises' were also enthusiastic supporters of land conservation and early benefactors of the National Trust. Much of the Lake District we see today owes its preservation to Beatrix and her husband. She bequeathed fifteen farms and more than 4,000 acres to the National Trust – a gift that protected and conserved the unique Lake District countryside. Her books, her art, her Herdwick sheep and her indomitable spirit are all part of her enormous legacy.

HAWKSHEAD

What can be said about Hawkshead, the beautiful and picturesque village where William Heelis practised? The premises he occupied was more recently a branch of Barclays Bank. An ancient institution in the village is

Hawkshead Grammar School, founded in 1585 and now a museum. Several famous scholars attended the school in former years. The habit of carving one's name in the surface of the school's wooden desks was popular among the pupils, and among those still visible today is that of William Wordsworth. Other notable scholars at the school were Dr Christopher Wordsworth, Master of Trinity College, Cambridge, the poet's brother; Dr Joshua King, President of Queens' College, Cambridge; Lord Brougham, Lord Chancellor of England and Edward Baines, politician and newspaper proprietor.

THE FURNESS RAILWAY AND THE WINDERMERE BRANCH LINE

When the various companies had completed a railway system around the coast from Carlisle to Lancaster, the Furness Railway Company quickly realised that there was a potential for personal travel and tourism because, for the first time, here was a fast and easy mode of transport for the masses. The Furness Railway, with an eye to the future, built a line from Plumpton Junction (near Ulverston) along the River Leven estuary to Greenodd. A final decision was then made to build an extension up the valley to Newby Bridge. The line, about 8 miles in length, was opened on 1 June 1869. The main revenue earner for the line was freight, coal for the Windermere steamers, iron ore for the Backbarrow Iron Works, and sulphur and saltpetre for the Black Beck and Low Wood gunpowder works. By 1872, the steamers of the United Windermere Steam Yacht

Company had been purchased outright by the Furness Railway but unfortunately, at the same time the iron ore industry started to decline and, with it, the fortunes of the Furness Railway. By 1900, with a more modern fleet of vessels on the lake, the Furness Railway was in an ideal position to encourage and carry train loads of day trippers and holidaymakers. The golden years of the branch had begun, and were to reach a peak just before the Great War, the traffic gradually tailing off as the motor car became more popular. By 1967, with the Beeching cuts and the closure of the ironworks, all services had ceased.

During the next six years there was an ongoing campaign to reopen the line as a private venture that met with many bureaucratic and other objections from British Rail, the Lake District Planning Board and a member of the public. It was only the persistence of enthusiasts and volunteers with the monetary support of Austin Maher, chairman and owner of the newly formed Lakeside and Haverthwaite Railway, that saw the line reopened on 2 May 1973 as a heritage railway. The train timetable links in with the Windermere steamer timetable between Ambleside, Bowness and Lakeside at the southern tip of Lake Windermere.

Going north again to the east side of the Helvellyn Range brings the reader to the Ullswater valley.

8

ULLSWATER AND THE SOUTH-EASTERN FELLS

ULLSWATER

The name of Ullswater is possibly due to the fact that the lake is situated among mountains, as *hul* in Saxon signified a mountain. However, it is more likely that that the name came from the Celtic *ulle*, meaning the bend or elbow.

Transport on Ullswater long ago: 'There is a comfortable inn at Pooley Bridge, on the foot of Ullswater, and another at Patterdale, a little distance from its head. They both furnish boats upon the lake, and the long wanted medium of land conveyance is now in part supplied. Horses and jaunting cars can be had at Pooley Bridge, and a post chaise and horses at Patterdale' (Jonathan Otley, 1834).

ECHOES OF ULLSWATER

A visitor attraction of the eighteenth-century at Ullswater was to 'try the echoes'. Vessels on the lake were armed with swivel guns and on a still evening, it was said, twenty-five distant reverberations could be heard from the discharge of a swivel with only 2oz of powder. Mr Hutchinson, in his *Excursion to the Lakes* p.65 describes one such event as follows:

> Whilst we sat to regale, the barge put off from shore to a station where the finest echoes were to be obtained from the surrounding mountains. The vessel was provided with six brass cannon mounted on swivels. On discharging one of these pieces, the report was echoed from the opposite rocks, where, by reverberation it seemed to roll from cliff to cliff, and return through every cave and valley, till the decreasing tumult gradually died away upon the ear.

The practice was continued in more recent times. Behind the Patterdale Hotel is a crag known at one time as Nell Crag. In the 1930s a cannon was occasionally fired from here to the great delight of the visitors.

THE ULLSWATER NAVIGATION AND TRANSIT COMPANY

For more than 100 years two nineteenth-century steam yachts have provided a regular service on the lake. *The Lady of the Lake,* the smaller of the two vessels, was launched in 1877, followed by *The Raven* in 1899. *The Raven*, built at Rutherglen near Glasgow, was carried in sections by rail to Penrith and then by horse dray to Pooley Bridge, where she was assembled. A passenger on *The Raven* in 1902 was the German Kaiser, who

The Raven *at Glenridding pier.*

was a guest of the famous Yellow Earl, Lord Lonsdale of Lowther.

In recent years the fleet has expanded to five vessels that now operate 363 days a year. At the time of writing (July 2017) *The Lady of the Lake* had celebrated 150 years of service on the lake.

GLENRIDDING VILLAGE AND FLOODING

The recent floodings of the Glenridding Hotel are, unfortunately, not just recent events. The dam storing water for Greenside lead mine up the valley was twice the cause of similar flooding. At 1.30 a.m. on Saturday, 29 October 1927, after a period of exceptional rainfall, the earthen wall of Kepple Cove Tarn dam burst, causing a great wall of water to descend on Glenridding far below. The size of the deluge was such that it left a gap in the dam 80ft wide by 60ft deep. The flood rushed down Glenridding Beck carrying away Rattle Beck Bridge, flooding houses alongside the beck and

Kepple Cove earth dam and the concrete dam.

Eagle Farm to a depth of 5 to 6ft. Debris, including dead sheep and a tea hut, was deposited on the other side of the lake near Side Farm. The basement bedrooms of the Glenridding Hotel were flooded and four sleeping girls floated up to the ceiling on their mattresses. One of these had a near escape as she was swept through a window, but was then saved by one Ernest Thompson. The peninsula at Glenridding, which is now the site of the steamer pier, was formed as a result of this flood, which also brought down a large mass of rocks with it. The rocks were used to build up this strip of land, which is now a popular recreation area for visitors. The Keppel Cove earth dam was replaced by a rough concrete dam that also burst, although less spectacularly, in 1931. Both dams are still to be seen to this day.

GREENSIDE MINE, GLENRIDDING (AND THE ATOMIC WEAPONS RESEARCH ESTABLISHMENT)

The mine probably opened during the second half of the 1700s but had closed by 1819. In 1825, the Greenside Mining Company was formed and reopened the mine, which became very successful. Between 1825 and 1961 the mine produced 159,000 tonnes of lead and 45 tonnes of silver. During the 1940s it was the largest producer of lead ore in the UK. Electricity was introduced in the 1890s, and it became the first metalliferous mine in Britain to use electric winding engines and an electric locomotive. The mine closed in 1962 after lead reserves had been exhausted.

In its long life Greenside Mine only suffered two major accidents, both occurring towards the end of its life. The first of these was due to a fire that started in the north shaft over the weekend, causing carbon monoxide to diffuse into the workings. On Monday, 7 July 1952, a group of miners were driven back by strong fumes as they approached the lift shaft, but not before hearing the shouts of miner Leo Mulyran, who had already descended to the bottom of the shaft. In the subsequent attempt to rescue him three men died, as did Mulyran himself. The heroic rescue attempt was recognised by justly deserved medals and commendations. The second fatal accident occurred in 1960 when the mine was about to close. The Atomic Energy Authority arranged to explode two charges of TNT, one of 500lb and the other of 250lb, in order to conduct seismic tests. The data was needed to calibrate instruments that would be used to monitor underground nuclear explosions. The charges were fired electrically from the surface but only the larger one went off. After the explosion the mine was ventilated and declared safe but two men, who later went in, were asphyxiated by an isolated pocket of gas trapped in one of the stopes. At the time the secrecy surrounding the project, and the involvement of the Atomic Energy Authority, led to rumours that a small atomic bomb had been exploded in the mine.

THE KING OF PATTERDALE

William Gilpin writing in 1772 said:

> Among the cottages of this village there is a house
> belonging to a person of somewhat better condition
> whose little estate, which he occupies himself, lies in the
> neighbourhood. As his property, inconsiderable as it is,
> is better than any of his neighbours, it has given him the
> title of 'King of Patterdale', in which his family name is
> lost. His ancestors have long enjoyed the title before him.

Gilpin was referring to the Mounsey family who
lived at Patterdale Hall. It was a Mounsey that led
the statesmen of Patterdale to victory, when, in the
narrow passage of the road between Ullswater and
the hill above they defeated a strong group of Scottish
raiders who had come to plunder their peaceful valley.
From then on the Mounseys were known as 'The Kings
of Patterdale'.

Wild goats of Patterdale – James Clarke in his *Survey
of the Lakes* (1789) quotes an amusing anecdote about
John Mounsey, last but one of the Kings of Patterdale.
He had a few goats on the hills that were wild and
very difficult to take. He sold four to a butcher for
two guineas and the butcher paid no less than thirty
shillings for catching them, and the takers had reason
to complain of their bargain.

Clarke also relates how Mr Mounsey made him a
present of some kids, on condition he catch them for
himself. He set out to do so next day with eleven men
and dogs. At last they cornered a goat in a craggy

position near Eusey (Aira) Force, from which there seemed to be no escape, but the goat charged the dog, which was attacking him, and fell with him over the precipice. The goat got up after the fall and got away, but the dog was killed.

Bad weather in Patterdale – If it is very windy in Patterdale and you are walking on Place Fell (the fell to the east of the village), then perhaps you should wear a safety helmet. Mrs Little records in *The Chronicles of Patterdale* (Women's Institute) how, on one very windy day in 1951, a corrugated iron garage, belonging to the White Lion Hotel in Patterdale, was blown to bits and pieces of the corrugated iron were scattered in and around the village. One piece soared higher than the rest and came down on Boredale Hause, halfway up Place Fell, having travelled a distance of about half a mile and achieved a vertical ascent of at least 800ft.

AIRA FORCE

Gowbarrow Park and Aira Force – This National Trust-managed area has a network of paths that meander through the woodland leading to the spectacular 65ft high Aira Force waterfall.

In the eighteenth century this area belonged to the Howards of Greystoke Castle, who renovated an old hunting lodge on the western shore of the lake at Gowbarrow. It was converted into a large building, Lyulph's Tower, complete with mock battlements and tower. The unusual name Lyulph's Tower probably relates to the Saxon owner of Greystoke Manor, who had the name Ulphus. One might also presume from this that the name of Ullswater was originally 'Ulf's Water'.

Later the area was landscaped around Aira Beck into a woodland garden with paths and bridges as seen today. In 1846 an arboretum was added. More than 200 specimen conifers (firs, pines, spruces and cedars) from all over the world were planted. One of these, a Sitka spruce, is now more than 118ft high. Wordsworth was inspired to compose his famous poem 'Daffodils' after encountering the flowers in profusion near the lakeside at Gowbarrow. He mentions Aira Force in three of his poems but the most famous is probably 'The Somnambulist', a legend of unrequited love.

MARTINDALE VALLEY

Martindale Old Church.

Martindale Old Church – Written records show the old church dates back to at least 1541. The ancient yew in the churchyard, now known to be 1,300 years old, indicates that there has been a church on this site for a very long time. The font is believed to have been a Roman altar brought down from the Roman road of High Street about 500 years ago.

THE AVARICIOUS RICHARD BIRKETT

James Clarke in his *Survey of the Lakes* (1789), remarks on the smallness of the stipend paid to the curate in Martindale in days gone by. In spite of this Richard Birkett, who served the curacy for sixty-seven years, amassed a considerable fortune. When he took up the post he was said to possess only two shirts and one suit of clothes. The 'living' consisted of an endowment of £2 15s 4d per annum (5p per week). A small house was provided with about 4 acres of land. Being the only person except one in the parish who could write, he transacted all the legal affairs of his 200 parishioners. Whenever he lent money he deducted, at the time of lending, interest at two shillings in the pound and the term of the loan never exceeded a year. Whenever he wrote a receipt he charged two pence and for a promissory note, fourpence and 'used such other acts of extortion as one would scarcely believe to have been practised in so contracted a sphere' (Clarke's words). He also served as parish clerk and was the local schoolmaster. In addition to his school fees he had a fortnight's free board and lodging at the house of each of his scholars and at Easter was paid in eggs. These he collected himself, carrying with him a board with a hole in it to serve as a gauge and 'he politely refused to accept any which would pass through'. This payment in kind was his 'Whittle Gate', as described earlier for 'Wonderful Walker'.

Although the living was only worth £17 a year, through his enterprise, economies and the exploitation of his parishioners, the Reverend Birkett was able to leave his wife £1,200 when he died.

MARTINDALE RED DEER HERD AND THE YELLOW EARL

The conical-shaped hill at the southern end of Mardale, where Bannerdale branches off to the right, is called the Nab. This is the home of the oldest herd of wild red deer in England and is the only pure red deer bloodstock in the country. The large red-roofed building called The Bungalow below the Nab was the shooting lodge used by the famous Yellow Earl of Lonsdale (Hugh Lowther) whose rather eccentric behaviour and capacity for spending money on sponsorship of good causes and on sport, made him a popular figure with the public at large, if not with the rest of the aristocracy. His interest in and sponsorship of boxing through the Sporting Club led to the creation of the famous Lonsdale Belt, the most desired prize in British boxing.

Hugh Lowther's lifelong liking for the colour yellow, which led to his nickname, was reflected in the livery of his large collection of carriages and later automobiles.

He was the first president of the Automobile Association and reputedly allowed it to use his livery on all its vehicles. The Yellow Earl entertained the Kaiser (the German Emperor) at Lowther Castle and at The Bungalow in 1895 and again in 1902. No expense was spared and Penrith was bedecked with bunting and decorations. The Kaiser arrived at Penrith railway station in the Earl's private, yellow-liveried train. Thousands of people converged on the town to cheer and to watch the extensive procession of troops and carriages from Penrith to Lowther Castle.

Apparently Lord Lowther believed in giving his guests good sport. He had heard that the Kaiser was partial to shooting rabbits and so arranged for his keepers to net as many rabbits as possible and hold them concealed in the wood where they were to shoot. As he approached the wood with the German emperor he is reported to have observed, 'We often find a rabbit or two in here' (or words to that effect). With that he gave orders for the dogs to be sent into the wood, whereupon his keepers released the captured rabbits. In a very short time rabbits were pouring out of the wood in their hundreds, rushing past the startled Kaiser, who was shooting away at them as fast as he could. This sort of prank was typical of the Yellow Earl. Hugh Lowther died in 1944, in his eighty-seventh year.

In recent years The Bungalow has been advertised for weekly let in a holiday catalogue as a large holiday residence. One of its stated attractions is the original Victorian decor and plumbing with large iron baths, etc.

MARDALE (THE DROWNED VALLEY)

The new road down the east side of the lake and the Haweswater Hotel (halfway along it) were built by the Manchester Corporation to provide access to the hills and accommodation for visitors after the flooding of the valley. The Haweswater Hotel is now a popular venue for visitors to the valley, which include coast to coast walkers, local hill walkers and eagle watchers, as well as those just wanting to enjoy the peace and quiet of this beautiful remote valley.

In 1919 the Manchester Corporation obtained parliamentary sanction to convert Haweswater into a reservoir. By 1925 it had bought out the landowners and taken possession of the land around the lake. The reservoir was brought into service in October 1941 and overflowed for the first time in December 1942. The dam raised the level of Haweswater by 96ft, trebling its surface area and increasing its capacity to 18,660 million gallons. The total cost of the dam was £476,948.

Unique in its day, the Haweswater dam is a hollow concrete buttress type of dam. It makes use of the immense compressive strength of concrete and was cheaper to build and is easier to maintain than the more traditional solid gravity dam. It can be inspected and maintained from within. Possible movement of the dam is monitored by a massive plumb bob hanging inside to indicate the vertical. This marker deflected one twentieth of an inch from the vertical when the dam first filled to overflowing in 1942.

Since that time Manchester's thirst for Lake District water has not abated, but the developments at Ullswater and Windermere have reflected the immense public concern to protect the National Park. Ullswater and Windermere pumping stations are underground, soundproofed and completely hidden. Both stations are remotely operated from the treatment works at Watchgate, north of Kendal. The Ullswater station, near Pooley Bridge, pumps water up the fellside to Tarn Moor tunnel, from where it flows to Heltondale and on to Haweswater. The Windermere station pumps water to a balancing reservoir at Banner Rigg, from where it flows to Watchgate. Several times since the flooding of the valley (most recently in 2014), when Haweswater was much lower than usual, roads, walls and a bridge of the drowned village have reappeared and walkers have been able to walk through the village once more.

THE BORDER REIVERS

These eastern fells provided corridors south for the marauding Scots and there are many tales of battles and skirmishes among these hills. Great Scarth Pass, Nan Bield Pass and High Street were frequently used. One such story describes how the burghers of Kendal received warning of an imminent Scottish raid. The raiders were expected to pass through Mardale by either Great Scarth or Nan Bield Pass. The men of Kendal laid a trap, posting their archers among the rocky ground on and surrounding Castle Crag on the west bank of Haweswater. When within shooting distance, the bowmen of Kendal poured volley after volley of arrows into the raiders, killing them all. The Scots were buried where they fell. The archers of Kendal were famed for their bravery. Besides covering themselves with glory at Agincourt they featured in the battle of Flodden Field:

> These were the bows of Kendale bold
> Who fierce will fight and never flee.

Incidentally, Castle Crag was probably no stranger to such violent happenings; like its namesake in Borrowdale, it is the site of an Iron Age fort.

How did the Border reivers come by their name? These warring families in the debatable lands widowed the wives of the men they slew. These wives were bereaved of their husbands. Hence the name.

The Corpse Road and Mardale Church – Prior to 1728, when Mardale Church was granted a licence for burials, baptisms and marriages, anyone who died in the dale had to be transported via the old corpse road to the parish church of Shap. The corpse road wends its way across the northern slopes of Selside Pike down into Swindale Head. The dead were strapped to the backs of fell ponies for the trip, as the route is rather a rough fell path and quite unsuitable for wheeled vehicles. On one such journey a wicked man, who had died in Mardale with an undivulged crime, was being carried over to Shap on the back of a strong young horse. During the journey a dreadful thunderstorm arose and the terrified horse bolted. For three months it roamed the fells, evading every attempt at capture. Then, as is usual in such tales, the secret came to light, the horse allowed itself to be caught and the poor man was buried at Shap where, hopefully, he rests in peace.

Today the corpse road is often used by walkers on the coast to coast route from St Bees to Robin Hood's Bay. As a result of the water scheme, the bodies at Mardale were exhumed and reburied; the majority of them at Shap. The church was demolished and some of its fittings distributed to other churches in the county. The bell went to St Barnabas, Carlisle, where it can still be heard today. The weathervane and various other artefacts went to Shap and the pulpit to Borrowdale. The stonework of the windows can still be seen, as it was incorporated into the upper chamber of the water intake well on the eastern shore of the lake.

HIGH STREET

This is the mountain ridge rising at Pooley Bridge and leading south towards Windermere that separates the Ullswater valley from the Haweswater valley. High Street probably derives its name from the 'strata' or Roman road that leads along it at more than 2,000ft above sea level. In the Middle Ages this path was used by the Border reivers on their forays into the district and was known as the Scots Rake.

This rather inhospitable place was surprisingly well frequented by the local inhabitants in times gone by. More than 150 years ago, on holidays and feast days, horse race meetings were held on the broad flat top above Blea Water, hence the name Racecourse Hill. Clarke in his *Survey of the Lakes*, describes how, on 10 July each year the shepherds of the area assembled here for: 'horse racing, wrestling, and other such like country

Horse racing on High Street in the past with Blea Water below.

diversions: hither, likewise, every one brings the stray sheep he has found during the preceding year, that they may be owned: they also at this time amuse themselves with fox hunting.'

He goes on to describe how at one such hunting a man called Dixon fell about 1,000ft from the top of Blea Water Crag. Although he hit the rocks several times on his way down, he had no broken bones, but was terribly bruised and was almost completely scalped. Dixon, a resident of Kentmere, survived to tell the tale and Clarke relates that the only hair on his head was a small tuft above one ear. The place on the crag where this unfortunate event occurred became known as Dixon's Three Jump.

Returning now to the central mountainous area of Cumbria south of Borrowdale and Buttermere, the road linking Seathwaite in Borrowdale to Buttermere climbs over Honister Pass.

9

HONISTER PASS AND THE CENTRAL SOUTHERN FELLS

HONISTER SLATE

Honister Pass is notable as being the site of England's only working slate mine. Slate has been mined at Honister for more than 300 years and over the last twenty years has become a developing tourist attraction with its 'Via Ferrata' routes and mine visits. The youth hostel at the summit of the pass was, in the past, accommodation for the mine workers. The workings here are massive, not only the surface workings but the underground cathedral-sized caverns.

Further back in time, before the mining of slate, the bones of the young Graeme, leader of one of the most notorious families of Border reivers, were buried here. The Graemes were renowned and feared for their predatory excursions into this remote corner of England. On one such raid they captured and drove away all the cattle and sheep they could find, via the Borrowdale–Honister route. Word spread quickly and the Dalesmen were soon in hot pursuit. The Graemes split into two groups, one party pushing forward with the captured booty while the rest waited in ambush in the rocks of Yew Crag and Honister, at the summit of the pass. The ambush party was led by the young Graeme and his aged father. When the English reached the neck of the pass the young Graeme sprang to his feet and waved his claymore at the enemy. Immediately volleys of musketry rang out from the crags and arrows flew through the air. The English leader was killed by a musket shot and fell from his horse. Furious at the loss of their leader, the troopers wheeled their horses round and stormed the crags on which the Graemes, and a few of their followers, were standing. Before help could arrive from the rest of the band the younger Graeme and several of his men were cut down. The English then dashed on down the pass away from the ambush point, still in pursuit of their sheep and cattle. The older Graeme was devastated by the loss of his son and heir. They laid his body to rest in an opening in the hillside and built a cairn of stones on top to mark the grave. Young Graeme's bonnet, shield and claymore were supposedly placed on top of the cairn 'that neither friend nor foe should thereafter pass it with irreverence'.

GREAT GABLE REMEMBRANCE SERVICE

Every year on Remembrance Sunday, whatever the weather, up to 500 people make their way to the top of Great Gable to observe the two-minute silence at the war memorial on the summit of the mountain. The majority of them start the ascent from the top of Honister Pass but some come from Seathwaite and from Wasdale Head.

The war memorial tablet on Great Gable was unveiled on Whit Sunday, 8 June 1924, by the Fell and Rock Climbing Club. The event was not only to record the installation of the memorial but also to celebrate the area being given to the National Trust.

W.T. Palmer reported as follows:

On Whit Sunday the Club completed its task of a permanent and magnificent memorial to members who fell in the Great War. In October, 1923, the title-deeds of 3,000 acres of high mountains had been handed over to the National Trust. The rocks, buttresses, and recesses of Lingmell, Great End, Allan Crags, Green Gable, Great Gable, Kirkfell and other peaks east and west of Sty Head Pass had been secured, as Dr. Wakefield (the new President) declared, 'to us and our children for ever'.

By far the best view from the summit of Gable is from Westmorland Cairn. The cairn lies directly above Westmorland Crags, about 130m south-west of the memorial. The cairn was built in 1879 by two brothers from Penrith of that name, who were of the opinion that it marked the best mountain viewpoint in that area.

From the summit of Gable to the south is the valley that climbs steeply from Seathwaite to Styhead Tarn and then descends into Wasdale, a wild, remote and beautiful area enjoyed by all. However, if planners had their way in the early twentieth century a road would have been built through here. Luckily the plan was opposed and shelved before it even got off the drawing board. An even earlier plan in the nineteenth century

The view down Wasdale from Westmorland Cairn.

was to extend the railway from Keswick down the Borrowdale valley to carry slate from Honister. That too was nipped in the bud by Canon Rawnsley and others. Later, Canon Rawnsley was a founding member of the National Trust.

MOSES' TROD AND THE SMUGGLER'S HUT ON GREAT GABLE

Moses' Trod, the well-known route that leads from Dubbs quarry to Great Gable and then down into Wasdale, has been associated with various forms of smuggling over the years. The path was used to ferry green slate on packhorses from Dubs to Wasdale and thence to Ravenglass for export. Moses Rigg, one of the quarrymen who used this route, was reputed to bring back a return load of smuggled goods from overseas for sale to the local populace. Another tale relates how Moses operated an illegal whisky still at Dubbs and used this route to export his product to his customers on the west coast. Yet another story says that stolen wad (graphite) from the Seathwaite mine, a very valuable commodity in the eighteenth century, was carried along this track into Wasdale. Whatever the truth of these tales, if smuggling did indeed occur, it follows that a remote, safe hideaway to store the goods en route would have been very useful. There were rumours that Moses had such a hideaway on Gable but nobody knew where it was. In 1890, according to Lakeland author O.S. MacDonell writing in *Cumbria* magazine, pioneer climber W.P. Haskett-Smith and two friends made a first ascent up the middle of Gable Crag. Near the top they came upon a stone building that they later named the Smuggler's Shelter. The hut is situated on a wide ledge below the summit, accessible with care from above but with great difficulty from below. The siting of the hut is such that it is almost impossible to see from anywhere but above and then only if one descends part of the way down the crag at the appropriate place. Today the hut is roofless and consists of a rectangular drystone wall built up against a rockface. Its purpose was possibly a

Smugglers shelter on Great Gable seen from above.

safe store for smuggled goods, which could be lowered from the summit of the crag. In particular wad, which had been pilfered from the mine at Seathwaite in small amounts by individuals, could be accumulated here until there was sufficient for a packhorse run along Moses' trod to Ravenglass. This would be a very lucrative business as wad commanded a price of £3,920 a ton in 1804. Another possible use of the hut, suggested by Graham Sutton in his book *Fell Days* was as a Jacobite refuge. If so, it was rather a remote refuge and it would have been rather difficult to keep the incumbent supplied with food, fuel and other necessary comforts for an extended stay.

WASDALE, SCAFELL PIKE AND AULD WILL RITSON

Scafell Pike is the highest mountain in England at 978m (3,208ft). It rises at the head of Wasdale, which is encircled by some of Lakeland's highest peaks. Rock climbing as a sport in England began in the 1880s when W.P. Haskett Smith scaled Napes Needle on Gable (to great publicity at the time).

By the turn of the century up to sixty budding climbers at a time would meet up at the Wastwater Hotel at the head of the valley. A local character was born in 1808 at Row Foot, Wasdale, later the Wastwater Hotel. Auld Will Ritson, as he became known, lived his whole life in the valley, becoming a guide to the many visitors who, thanks to Wordsworth and other early writers of Lake District guides, now 'discovered the sublime beauties of

Napes Needle on the Gable traverse.

the crags and precipices of that wonderful valley'. Will was renowned for his ready wit and soon became very popular with tourists who placed themselves in his charge. His remark to a clergyman who he was conducting to the top of Scafell Pike was typical of this humour. As they neared the summit he said, 'Tha'lt ne'er be nigher t' heaven than now.'

Auld Will Ritson.

Will eventually married and set up as innkeeper at Row Foot, which later became the Huntsman's Inn. Will became friendly with Professor Wilson, alias Christopher North (mentioned earlier in the story of John Gough). Both Will and Wilson were athletic men and the pair soon became renowned for their practical jokes, rude horseplay and rough behaviour. Will related how Wilson wanted to go out on the lake for a sail with him and friends:

Then nowt would sarra but he would hev a boat an' they must all hev a sail. Well, when they gat into t'boat he tell'd em to be particularly careful, for he was liable to get giddy I' t' head, an' if yan of his giddy fits sud chance to come he mud happen tumble into t' water. Well, that pleased 'em all gaily weel, an' they said they'd tak vary girt care on him. Then he leaned back an' called oot that they must pull quicker. So they did an' what does Wilson do then but tipples ower eb'm of his back I' t' watter wi' a splash. Then there was a girt cry: 'Eh Maister Wilson's I' t' watter!' An' yan clickt an' anudder, but nean o' them could get hod on him. An' there was sic a scrow as nivver was. At last yan o' them gat him round the neck as he popped up, at t' teal o' t' boat, an Wilson toad him to keep a good hod, for he mud happen slip back agean. But what, it was nowt but his bits o' prank – he was smirkin an' laughin' all t' time.

Will Ritson was renowned for his wit and his tall tales. After all, Wasdale was home to the deepest lake, the highest mountain, and the smallest church. He claimed the turnips in Wasdale were so big that, after the dalesfolk had quarried into them for Sunday lunch, they could be used as sheds for the sheep. With many tales like this Will was the founder of the 'Biggest Liar' competition, which is still held every November at the Bridge Inn, Santon Bridge. In 2008, John 'Johnny Liar' Graham of Causewayhead Silloth won the competition for the seventh time after telling the judges a story of a magical ride to Scotland in a wheelie bin that went under the sea.

CORPSE ROAD TO ESKDALE, BURNMOOR, GHOSTS AND MORE STONE CIRCLES

A path from Wasdale Head leads south up to Burnmoor past the tarn and down to Boot in Eskdale. In times past, before the churchyards of Wasdale had been consecrated, this was the route taken by funeral corteges with the coffin strapped on to the back of a horse. The road led to St Catherine's Church at Boot. On one such journey, for the funeral of a young man, the horse took fright and bolted, being lost by the mourners in the mist. The young man's mother fretted and died, and at her funeral, which took place on a snowy day, the horse bearing the coffin was lost like that which bore her son. The searchers followed the tracks in the snow, subsequently found the first horse and duly carried out the son's funeral. The mother's corpse, however, was never recovered and her weary spirit still haunts the hillside. So, if walking over Burnmoor in the mist, do not be surprised if a galloping horse suddenly appears with a dark object on its back. It is only the poor lad's mother trying to find a resting place for her soul. Careful readers will note that in other parts of this book two other corpse roads have been mentioned, one of which had a similar ghostly story attributed to it. The writer cannot vouch for the truth or otherwise of these tales. They have been passed down from generation to generation and are recorded here for posterity.

Burnmoor has long featured in local history and folklore of the district, and relics of its former importance are still to be found. In spite of its remoteness it was populated at a very early period. Evidence for this is provided by the large number of stone barrows or burial mounds. On Burnmoor the remains usually consist of stone circles. The largest of these consists of forty-one stones and has a diameter of 100ft (30.5m). It encloses five burial mounds, each of which is said to have contained a box built up of five stones, which contained burnt bones together with horns of stags and other animals. According to McIntyre, the small size and irregular settings of the stones of these circles would indicate that they were merely 'taboo rings' to mark the limits of the sepulchre, or to keep the ghosts of the departed from wandering from his or her tomb to haunt the living. Burnmoor was a great meeting place long ago. At the feast of Beltane in May each year men from the neighbouring valleys of Wasdale, Eskdale and Mitredale would meet to light their fires and celebrate Beltane. They would drive their stock through the smoke for 'good luck', to drive out the devil and see an end to the winter. The smoke would probably have a useful effect on the parasites on the animals as well.

THE CONISTON AREA

The A593 from Ambleside leads one south-west to Coniston, a small town at the head of Coniston Water. Once an industrial centre for the quarrying of slate and copper mining, its main industry now is tourism. At its height Coniston Copper Mine employed around 400 people, mainly Irish immigrant miners and their families. Most of the remaining surface and underground workings date back to the nineteenth century, the most profitable era for the mine. The ore was transhipped by barge to the foot of the lake and then carted to Greenodd for shipment to the Swansea smelter. From 1859, when the railway arrived at Coniston, the ore was taken by rail to Barrow for transhipment to the smelter. Unfortunately, in the late nineteenth century the increasing availability of cheap supplies of copper from

Coppermines Valley, Coniston, as seen today.

DAVID LUSH

abroad spelt the death knell of the industry, and, by 1900 copper mining had effectively ceased at Coniston.

Apart from the extensive industrial history, Coniston is famous for Brantwood, the home of John Ruskin for many years. Ruskin, poet, writer, artist, art critic, philosopher and social reformer, was famous before he came to Brantwood in 1872, aged 53. He had fallen in love with the Lake District mountains when visiting with his parents in 1833. The poetry he wrote at the time showed he missed nothing and was entranced by the beauty of the area. Canon Rawnsley in his book *Ruskin and the English Lakes* published in 1902, describes this well: 'he gazes back upon the Coniston lake, is struck by the beauty of rain cloud and mist-hidden shores, and notes the way in which "The mountains all mistily softened away – Appeared like thin clouds at the dawn of the day." It is not great poetry truly, but it shows accuracy in observation, and the boy's heart is full to overflowing.'

Something of a child prodigy, John was an avid reader by the age of 5 and was writing his own verse and prose by the age of 7. He travelled widely in Europe in his earlier years, visiting Germany, Switzerland, Italy and France. Here his love of the mountains came to the fore. In spite of the grandeur of the European Alps he still loved the English Lake District above all else. It was mainly his inspiration that led Canon Rawnsley to put forward his

John Ruskin in 1864 [drawn by Samuel Lawrence].

paper entitled 'The Proposed Permanent Lake District Defence Society' in 1833, the first step towards forming the National Trust. This initiative came about as a direct result of the continued attempts by the railway companies to obtain parliamentary permission for new lines into the district. These had been all strongly resisted by Wordsworth, Ruskin, Rawnsley and others. Rawnsley presented his paper shortly after the successful defeat of a proposal to build a railway from Braithwaite to Honister, known at the time as the Braithwaite–Buttermere Railway. This line would have traversed Cat Bells and Maiden Moor, passing between Castle Crag and High Spy on its way to the head of Borrowdale and the Slate Quarries. Thankfully, like several other proposals such as the Yanwath–Pooley Bridge line and the Ennerdale line, it was never built, due mainly to the efforts of these early conservationists.

SIR DONALD CAMPBELL AND CONISTON

Sir Donald Campbell CBE became closely associated with the Lake District through his various attempts at world water speed records on Coniston Water and to a lesser extent on Ullswater. In January 1949, Campbell heard that Henry Kaiser was building a boat to regain the world water speed record for America. At the time the record was held by Donald's father, Sir Malcolm Campbell, who had achieved a speed of 141.74mph in August 1939, shortly before his death from a heart attack. Donald wanted to retain the record for Britain and in the next sixteen years he was to increase the world water speed record no fewer than seven times. Then, in 1950, the American Stanley Sayers, raised the record to 176mph. Campbell then set about raising money for a jet-powered Bluebird and his efforts paid off when, in 1955, he raised the record to 202.32mph on Ullswater. He quickly followed this success by raising the record to 216.2mph on Lake Mead in Nevada.

About this time, when everything was going well, Campbell suggested building a Bluebird car to travel at more than 400mph and break John Cobb's land speed record of 394mph. Whilst this was being developed he returned to Coniston Water where, during the next four years, he broke his own record four more times, raising the water speed record to 260.35mph by 1959.

On 16 September 1960 the car was trialled at Bonneville Salt Flats, Utah, where it crashed on its fifth run. Campbell had the car rebuilt and, after many problems and delays, he finally raised the land speed record to 403mph on 17 July 1964. Then, on the last day of the year, on Lake Dumbleyung in Australia, he broke the world water speed record once again with a speed of 276.3mph in Bluebird. This feat made him the first person in history to have broken both land and water speed records within the space of one year.

A world water speed record of 300mph was now within reach. He returned to Coniston and between November 1966 and January 1967 made several further attempts on the record. It was on the last of these, on 4 January 1967, that he tragically met his death. Campbell had just completed a successful first run at almost 300mph. He turned for the second run and, instead of waiting for the lake to settle down again, set off within four minutes of the first run. During the second run down the lake Bluebird rose out of the water, somersaulted and crashed. On 28 January 1967, Campbell was posthumously awarded the 'Queen's Commendation for Brave Conduct' for his courage and determination in attacking the world water speed record. Between them, Donald Campbell and his father had set eleven speed records on water and ten on land.

The farmland of Cumbria extends well to the east of the Lakeland Fells and up on to the Pennines (known as the backbone of England) in places. Several market towns are scattered over this area, which are described in alphabetical order beginning with Alston.

10

MARKET TOWNS TO THE EAST OF THE LAKELAND FELLS

ALSTON

This small market town in the North Pennines in an area of outstanding beauty is historically part of Cumberland. Alston shares the dubious title of the 'highest market town in England' along with Buxton in Derbyshire (300m or 1,000ft). The name of the town is recorded in 1164–71 as Aldeneby and in 1209 as Aldeneston, and seems to mean 'the settlement or farmstead belonging to Halfdan (a Viking name)'. In the past lead mining was a major industry in the area and in the thirteenth century the area was known as the silver mines of Carlisle.

Silver is found in a high proportion (up to 40 ounces per long ton, or 1.2 g/kg of smelted lead) and was used to create coinage in the Royal Mint, established in Carlisle for the purpose. Most mining was very small scale until the mid-eighteenth century. The biggest mine owner in the area was the London Lead Company; a Quaker organisation, with enlightened employment policies. In 1745, it began construction of a school, a library, a sanitary house, a surgeon's house, a market hall with clock tower, a laundry and a 'ready money' shop in Nenthead 4 miles away.

Many of the last mines closed in the 1950s. A small drift coal mine (Ayle Colliery) was still active in 2013. The main industry now is tourism, the largest attraction being the South Tynedale Railway, a narrow gauge railway and heritage centre. This runs from Alston along part of the closed line that, in the past, linked Haltwhistle to Alston. In a good winter one can ski not far from here, 7 miles down the road at Yad Moss is the Carlisle Ski Club's ski tow.

APPLEBY

Appleby has been called Appleby in Westmorland since 1974, when the new county of Cumbria was formed. The local council effected a change in the town's name to preserve the old county name. Appleby has a castle dating back to Norman times. In the seventeenth century the castle was the home of Lady Anne Clifford. The Clifford family estates in northern England were vast, and included five great castles in Westmorland and Yorkshire. Anne's two brothers died young, and as the only surviving child of the 3rd Earl, she might have expected to succeed to the estates when he died in 1605. But instead he left them to his brother, Francis, and to Francis's heirs. In doing so he had breached an entail dating back to the early fourteenth century, under which they should have passed to the eldest heir, whether male or female – which was Anne.

Anne would not accept this state of affairs, which led to an interminable legal battle against her uncle, and later his son Henry, which was only resolved many years later when Henry died.

The last three decades of Lady Anne's life were highly creative. The estates were badly neglected and the five Clifford castles – Brough, Brougham, Appleby and Pendragon in Westmorland and Skipton Castle in Yorkshire – were ruined or in poor condition. Pendragon had been abandoned since the reign of Edward III, and Brough since a devastating fire there in 1521, which had left 'nothing ... but the bare walls standing'. The other castles had been damaged during the Civil War.

Gradually, Lady Anne restored her estates, and repaired all five castles. Conscious of their antiquity, she took great pains to restore them in a style in keeping with what was already there.

APPLEBY HORSE FAIR

Appleby has become famous for its annual horse fair, held in early June, that brings gypsies and travellers from all over Britain to the town. The earliest record of the fair is in the twelfth century, with a charter from Henry II, but it is believed to have a longer tradition than that.

Appleby is on the Settle–Carlisle line, opened in 1876 and still running to this day. The other major line through the town was the South Durham and Lancashire Union Railway route across the Pennines, notorious for snow blockages in winter, with a summit height of 1,370ft (417m) above sea level. This was the highest point of the railway in England until the line was closed in stages between 1952 and 1962. A short section of this line at Kirkby Stephen East has been restored by the Stainmore Railway Company.

BRAMPTON IN CUMBRIA

This small, picturesque market town lies only 3km south of Hadrian's Wall and Lanercost Priory, built between 1165 and 1174. Much of the stone for the priory came from Hadrian's Wall and there are several stones with Roman inscriptions to be seen in its walls. The priory was a target of Scots attacks in retaliation to English raids. In 1296 the Scottish army encamped at Lanercost after burning Hexham Priory and Lambley nunnery. Longshanks (Edward I) made several visits to the priory in the latter part of his reign, the last of which, in 1307, lasted five months, putting a huge burden upon the resources of the priory. It was while Edward was at Lanercost that the brothers of Robert de Brus and other Scottish captives were sent to Carlisle for execution by his order. His final journey after this visit is described in the section on Carlisle in this book.

BIRDOSWALD FORT

A few miles further east from Lanercost, following Hadrian's Wall is Birdoswald Fort (original name Banna, Latin for 'spur' or 'tongue' as it is on high ground and protudes above a sharp meander in the River Irthing). This is one of the best preserved of the sixteen forts along Hadrian's Wall, probably due to its remote location. An interesting piece of Roman graffiti can be seen carved on a stone, at eye level on Hadrian's Wall, a short distance east of the fort on the south side. It may be described as a Roman 'good luck' symbol, as it features the reproductive parts of the male anatomy.

The 2-mile sector of Hadrian's Wall either side of Birdoswald is currently the only known sector of Hadrian's Wall in which the original turf wall was later replaced by a stone wall on a different line. When the rebuilding took place (probably in the 130s) the line of the wall was moved approximately 50m further north, to line up with the fort's north wall, rather than its east and west gates.

BROUGH IN WESTMORLAND

Brough in Westmorland (sometimes referred to as Brough under Stainmore) was an important place in Roman times. The village is on the site of the Roman fort of Verterae on the northern leg of the Roman Watling Street, which linked Carlisle with York. The Norman castle at Brough was built in the eleventh century within the northern part of the former fort.

KENDAL

Kendal in the south of the county, like many of the larger settlements in Cumbria, was occupied by the Romans from the first to the fourth century and they built a fort at Watercrook, south of the modern town. The Normans followed, building a castle west of the town on Castle Hill around 1183. In 1189, Kendal was granted its Market Charter and is a market town to this day. Kendal, down in the valley, was bypassed initially by the railway. A 2-mile (3.5km) tunnel north of Kendal had been proposed to allow the Lancashire and Carlisle Railway to be routed via the town, but that was too expensive and the line seen today, running 1.5km east of Kendal, was built. As a result, efforts were put towards a branch line from Oxenholme, to run through Kendal to Windermere. Against a lot of opposition, as described elsewhere in this book, the line to Kendal was constructed in time for the opening of the main line southwards from Oxenholme in September 1846. Then in April 1847, the through route to Windermere station, at Birthwaite, was opened.

Nowadays Kendal is mainly a tourist town with its Kendal Calling festival and its famous mint cake, Kendal mint cake, which is based on a traditional recipe known as mint cake, peppermint tablet, and various other names. The origin of the cake is allegedly the result of a batch of peppermint creams that went wrong. Supposedly, the mixture was left overnight and it solidified. The 'mint cake' was then discovered in the morning.

Kendal mint cake has been used on many expeditions around the world as a source of energy. Sir Edmund

Hillary and his team carried Romney's Kendal Mint Cake with them on the first successful attempt on Mount Everest in 1953. The packaging currently includes the following: 'We sat on the snow and looked at the country far below us ... we nibbled Kendal Mint Cake.' A member of the successful Everest expedition wrote: 'It was easily the most popular item on our high altitude ration – our only criticism was that we did not have enough of it.' Mint cake was provided for the imperial Trans-Antarctic Expedition (1914–17), which was led by Sir Ernest Shackleton. Ewan McGregor and Charley Boorman included mint cake in their supplies for their 2004 motorcycle trip around the world and Kendal mint cake is also a standard part of the twenty-four-hour ration pack issued to the Irish Defence Forces.

KIRKBY STEPHEN

Kirkby Stephen is another small market town in Cumbria served by the Settle–Carlisle Railway. The town is on the line of Wainwright's Coast to Coast Walk and is a popular base for walkers in the Eden valley. In June there is the Mallerstang Horseshoe and Nine Standards Yomp, which takes a strenuous route on the high ground along both sides of the neighbouring dale of Mallerstang, including Wild Boar Fell and Nine Standards Rigg.

It is sometimes said that Faraday Road (parallel with High Street and Market Street) is named in honour of the scientist, Michael Faraday (1791–1867). Actually it is named after his uncle, Richard Faraday, who was a respected local tradesman. Richard's younger brother, James, was for some time the blacksmith in nearby Outhgill but his famous third child, Michael, was born soon after they had moved to London. The Faraday brothers moved from Clapham in the West Midlands to the Kirkby Stephen area because the family were members of the Sandemain Sect, and one of the few Sandemanian communities with a chapel was based locally.

MILLOM

The name Millom is Cumbrian dialect for 'at the mills'. The town was built as a new town, beginning in 1866. It was built around ironworks and grew to a population of more than 10,000 by the 1960s, but the works were closed in 1968 and today the population is about 7,000. Millom is notable as the birthplace of poet Norman Nicholson and as a major centre of amateur rugby league.

PENRITH

Penrith has a rich history. Penrith Castle was built between 1399 and 1470 as a defence against Scottish raiders and is thought to be built on the site of a Roman fort. The town was granted a market charter in 1223 by Henry III. William Wordsworth spent much of his childhood in Penrith, attending the Dame School run by Anne Birkett. The building overlooks the beautiful St Andrews Church and is probably the earliest example of a residential residence in Penrith. One of the most

The Giant's Grave.

interesting artefacts in Penrith is the Giant's Grave or Giant's Thumb in St Andrews churchyard, the legend of which is described in the story of King Dunmail elsewhere in this book.

Efforts to attract tourism to the town in earlier times may be found in the name of another monument. Just outside Penrith at Eamont Bridge is King Arthur's Round Table. This is a monument that dates back to the Iron Age (3,000 to 5,000 BC), being a prehistoric circular earthwork bounded by a ditch and an outer bank. Several hundred years ago towns all over the country were claiming to be the home of King Arthur, both for the prestige and for attracting visitors to their area. Another example is Arthuret Church near Longtown.

Not far from here is another thirteenth-century castle. Brougham Castle was built on the site of a Roman fort, at the intersection of three Roman roads. The great keep largely survives, amid many later buildings including the unusual double gatehouse. Like Penrith Castle, it was

Long Meg and her Daughters.

built as a formidable barrier against Scots invaders and was also a prestigious residence. The castle welcomed Edward I in 1300.

East of Penrith near Little Salkeld are Long Meg and her Daughters, a Bronze Age stone circle, the sixth-biggest example known from this part of north-western Europe.

Maybe we are lucky that they are still there as Lieutenant Colonel Samuel Lacy of nearby Salkeld Hall was once infamous for attempting to blow up the stones with gunpowder. However, commencement of the work coincided with a violent thunderstorm, which was interpreted by the workers as a supernatural warning and they refused to continue the work. Thereafter Lacy had a change of heart. However, Lacy is responsible for a more modern visitor attraction. Lacy's caves are man-made caves, originally created as a decorative folly in the 1800s. They consist of five chambers carved out of the sandstone rocks directly above the River Eden at Glassonby, to the north of Little Salkeld.

SHAP

The remote village of Shap is situated high in the dales east of the Lakeland fells on the old A6 road. Shap was a busy place in the past, being the last major stopping point before the dreaded Shap Summit at 1,350ft above sea level. The A6 across Shap summit formed the main north–south route, linking the industrial areas of north-west England with Scotland. It was busy, and notoriously hazardous in poor weather conditions. Often in winter the road became snowbound and impassable. Ironically, when the M6 arrived, it spelt disaster for many of the prosperous shops, hotels and other businesses on which the economy of the village relied. The railway came to Shap in 17 December 1846, but the station was closed in 1968, though there have been recent calls for its reopening.

People have lived here for many thousands of years. The area around the village was extensively settled in Neolithic times, and there are several stone circles, and other standing stones nearby. In the eighteenth, nineteenth and early twentieth centuries such artefacts were obviously not considered as important as they are now. The Kemp Howe Stone Circle, a short distance south of the village, is cut in two by the railway, narrowly missed by the A6 and overshadowed by the limeworks. Only six stones remain, with others probably under the railway embankment, and those that were on the other side of the railway now lost after construction of the works sidings. This circle used to have an avenue of stones leading from it in a north-north-westerly direction to a barrow. Some of these can still be seen today, although the avenue was ruined at the time of enclosure of the common land. Just to the west of Shap are dotted a collection of standing stones that are the remains of this avenue.

Shap Abbey is about half a mile west of the village. It was built in 1199, the last abbey to be founded in England, and the last to be dissolved by Henry VIII in 1540. One passes it on the Wainwright Coast to Coast Walk, having come across from Mardale (the drowned valley) via Swindale and the Corpse Road.

Today Shap is famous for its quarries. Shap blue granite, and the more famous Shap pink granite, seen throughout Britain in kerbstones and building frontages are both quarried near here. Shap Beck Limestone Quarry is quite close to the granite quarries. The limestone originates from sediments that were deposited in a tropical sea that was the first to flood across the slates and granites of Cumbria around 400 million years ago. Most of the crushed limestone is used in the large-scale production of lime for steelmaking.

About 5km south of the village is Shap Wells Hotel, opened in 1833 to serve the growing numbers of visitors coming to take the waters of the Shap Spa, located in the hotel's grounds. Under the ownership of the Earl of Lonsdale the hotel became a fashionable resort visited by many members of the aristocracy, the best known of these being HRH Princess Mary. During the Second World War, Shap Wells was requisitioned as a prisoner of war camp for senior Luftwaffe and German naval officers. Now it's a country house hotel.

TEBAY

In Roman times the small village of Tebay lay on a road linking a fort at Low Borrow Bridge near Tebay with one south of Kirkby Lonsdale. However, in more recent times, Tebay was on the Lancaster and Carlisle Railway, built between 1844 and 1846. Then in 1861 Tebay became an important junction, when the Stainmore Railway came into the village from Kirkby Stephen. The railway companies provided much employment for local people, the population increased and more housing was built.

In recent years two railway accidents happened nearby. On 15 February 2004, four people working on the line were run over and killed by a maintenance vehicle. A wagon laden with lengths of steel rail ran away from a maintenance location on the line because of faulty brakes. Three years later, the Grayrigg accident happened between Oxenholme and Tebay. Unfortunately one passenger, 84-year-old Margaret Masson from Glasgow, died later in hospital.

THE WITCH OF TEBAY

The Cross Keys public house in the village is associated with the ghost of Mary Baynes, known as the Witch of Tebay, who lived here until the age of 90, dying in 1811. The story says she was feared by the locals for forecasting the coming of the railway (that which she called 'fiery horseless carriages'). She was also supposed to have hexed a local farmhand who didn't give her cat a proper burial after it was killed by the Cross Keys' dog. It was said she died because eggs she cursed were fried. Now apparently haunting the inn, she has been seen in a blue dress climbing into a bed, borrowing objects and playing with lights.

ULVERSTON

Ulverston is an old market town with cobbled streets and, although inland from the sea, became an official port with the opening of the 2km-long Ulverston Canal in 1796. Over the years the town has been the birthplace of several famous people including Sir John Barrow, a former Admiralty second secretary, apparently a much more important position than first secretary. The Hoad monument that stands high above the town was built to commemorate him in 1850. It is a replica of the third Eddystone lighthouse.

Other well-known and not so well-known former citizens are comedian Stan Laurel (of Laurel and Hardy fame), Maude Green (mother of Bill Haley), Norman Gifford (England test cricketer), Francis Arthur Jefferson (awarded the Victoria Cross) and Bryan Martin, senior BBC Radio 4 newsreader. In 1977, Bryan Martin announced the death of Elvis Presley on the *Today* programme and broke the news of the Iranian Embassy siege in 1980. He appeared in the *News Quiz*, occasionally introduced *The Goon Show* and read the spoof news bulletin that always featured in the comedy *The Men from the Ministry*.

The Hoad Monument.

ACKNOWLEDGEMENTS

Much of the material for this book came from previous books that I have researched and/or published over the last twenty years. The sources I used were often lodged in the Cumbria Archive at Carlisle, and the Carlisle Library, particularly the Jackson library. My thanks go to all of those archive and library staff who have helped me over the years, particularly Stephen White at Carlisle Library.

My good friend and local historian Denis Perriam, with whom I have published several books in recent times, has been a fount of knowledge and is responsible for much of the original research in those books.

More recently, of course, for the parts of Cumbria not covered in my previous publications, much of my research has been done on the internet using websites of local organisations such as Cumbria Tourism, Cumbrian town councils, local history groups, Mine Explorer Society, Beatrix Potter Society, Ian Tyler, Hawkshead Grammar School Museum, The Theatre by the Lake website and, of course, Wikipedia. Their online information and links are very much appreciated.

Several items of information have come from books I have published for their authors such as Peter Ostle, Stephen Wright, Patricia Hitchon, Dennis Donald,